To Rick,

Christmas

Always take time
to smell the roses &
make your surroundings
as special as you are.

Love
Jon

THE WAYSIDE GARDENS COLLECTION

The WELL-PLANNED GARDEN

THE WAYSIDE GARDENS COLLECTION

The WELL-PLANNED GARDEN

A Practical Guide to Planning & Planting

Rupert Golby

John E. Elsley, General Editor for The Wayside Gardens Collection

Sterling Publishing Co., Inc.   New York

Library of Congress Cataloging-in-Publication Data

Golby, Rupert.
    The well-planned garden : a practical guide to plan-
ning & planting / Rupert Golby.
       p.   cm. — (The Wayside Gardens collection)
    Includes index.
    ISBN 0-8069-4266-5
    1. Gardens—Design.   I. Title.   II. Series.
SB473.G577   1995
712'.6—dc20   95–32220
                                          CIP

2 4 6 8 10 9 7 5 3 1

Published 1996 by Sterling Publishing Company, Inc.

387 Park Avenue South, New York, N.Y. 10016

The Wayside  Gardens Collection edition

© 1996 Conran Octopus Limited
The original edition first published
in Great Britain by Conran Octopus Limited
37 Shelton Street, London WC2H 9HN
Text and original planting schemes © 1994 by Rupert Golby
Design and layout © 1994 by Conran Octopus Limited
Distributed in Canada by Sterling Publishing
℅ Canadian Manda Group, One Atlantic Avenue, Suite 105
Toronto, Ontario, Canada M6K 3E7
Printed and bound in Hong Kong
All Rights Reserved

American Project Editor	Hannah Steinmetz
Project Editor	Jane O'Shea
Project Art Editor	Ann Burnham
Editor	Carole McGlynn
Designer	Alistair Plumb
Picture Researcher	Helen Fickling
Editorial Assistant	Caroline Davison
Production	Clare Coles
Illustrators	Shirley Felts
	David Ashby
	Vanessa Luff
	Valerie Price
	Michael Shoebridge

Sterling ISBN 0-8069-4266-5

FRONT JACKET Lavandula *'Hidcote' complements the
subtle colors of this path leading farther into the
garden.*

BACK JACKET Buddleia *'White Cloud' lends height to
the colorful flower beds that help this house and
garden to merge together.*

PAGE 1 *A stone lion on a base is framed by an arch
in a beech hedge.*

PAGE 2 *An enclosed garden on two paved levels is
connected by a flight of steps. Clematis, roses and
ivies clothe the walls.*

RIGHT *A tunnel framed by yew hedging is overhung
by stilted and trained London plane trees.*

CONTENTS

What makes a well-planned garden?   7

Planning the garden layout   13

The vertical dimension   27

The horizontal dimension   59

Embellishing the garden   93

Through the seasons   103

*Key plants for the
well-planned garden*   109

Index   124

Acknowledgments   128

WHAT MAKES A WELL-PLANNED GARDEN?

All gardens are different. They vary greatly in size and shape and in the ingredients which make them up. There is no recipe for a well-planned garden—indeed, in many cases it is a garden's uniqueness that makes it special. But careful thought at the planning stage will reward you, year after year, with the satisfaction of having a garden that meets all your needs and that works well, practically as well as visually.

This confined corner of a garden in high summer has all the appeal of a charming outdoor room. The seat on a terrace is surrounded by the luxuriant growth of sun-loving climbing plants. The banksian rose (Rosa banksiae 'Lutea') showers deep primrose-colored clusters of flowers, some falling onto the sapphire-blue Ceanothus 'Cascade.' The bearded iris links harmoniously with the yellow rose. The natural stone path, fringed and colonized by low-growing plants, offers a dry place to sit all year round.

If a garden has been carefully thought out and well designed, it not only looks pleasing, with a strong layout, harmonious materials and attractive planting, but it works. This is to say that the paths are in the right place, the terrace is afforded some shade, the utilitarian areas of the garden are screened off and, if appropriate, there is somewhere for young children to play. Whatever the components of the garden, there should be a logical progression through the garden and a theme tying the whole together, be it a certain material, color or style of planting.

Whether you are creating a garden from scratch, or modifying an existing one, it is vital to devote enough time to the important preliminary stages of forethought, research and planning. Mistakes are all too often made, or inappropriate decisions taken, which could have been avoided if the options had been fully explored at the initial stage. It is dangerous to narrow your mind early on, as interesting opportunities may all too easily be overlooked, only to be recalled when it is too late.

Forethought involves deciding what you expect from the garden and how you will use it. It implies a consideration of the materials you will use—for paving, walls and hedges—as well as the main plants. Today there is a greater range of materials available than ever before, which provides an exciting choice—but at the same time such a wide range can baffle the inexperienced and it becomes difficult to know where and how to start making decisions. Besides questions of cost, appropriateness and personal taste, you should bear in mind the local climate when selecting materials, and choose something that will prove long-lasting and resilient.

I place great emphasis on the importance of research, which to my mind lies in critically observing other properties, where positive and negative lessons may be learned at first hand. Once you start

The strong architectural lines of precisely clipped yew hedging can be breathtakingly beautiful when the hedge plants are mature. The contrasting shapes formed by the individual trees, particularly the weeping pear and the cherry clothed in its spring blossom, seem to accentuate the formality of the hedging.

BELOW *The author is seen in his own Oxfordshire garden in late summer, next to the white mophead flowers of* Hydrangea arborescens *'Annabelle,' teasels* (Dipsacus fullonum) *and the purple-flowered* Malva sylvestris.

RIGHT *Dividing a garden into compartments allows different themes or at least a change of atmosphere to be created. Through this darkened doorway clad with* Actinidia deliciosa, *with* Lonicera nitida *'Baggesen's Gold' at ground level, the open door reveals an enticing glimpse of the garden beyond, bathed in sunlight. The gravel path leading into the distance is softened by mounds of brightly colored catmint (*Nepeta *'Six Hills Giant').*

looking around, you will soon recognize materials, building styles and designs that are in sympathy with their surroundings—and additions of inappropriate style and materials even quicker. This is not a question of taste, good or bad, for taste, like beauty, is in the eye of the beholder. It is a matter of respect for existing features—the surrounding landscape or other buildings—and working with, rather than against, what you have. This does not mean that we should slavishly reproduce and restore every garden back to its presumed origins, for some of the finest gardens have been made over a long period and owe their beauty to a succession of stages which time has helped to unite. But the use of sympathetic materials or period features will significantly ease a newly designed or redesigned garden into its context.

Developing the plan

In working out a ground plan for the garden, you should aim for a balanced ratio between hard landscape areas, such as paths, terraces and drives, and the soft, planted areas made up of lawns, shrub beds and herbaceous borders. Both hard and soft surfaces have to fulfill practical roles, such as paths providing dry routes through the garden in winter and a terrace furnished comfortably as a sitting-out area for meals and relaxation. Lawns should always be considered carefully, no matter how small the garden, for they provide a unique, bland surface against which both plants and paving can be shown to good effect. The overall layout should link the hard and soft areas, the trees, shrubs and flower borders together harmoniously, so that the garden has a natural flow.

Planning a garden is in some respects like designing the interior of a house—involving both structural divisions and decorations—but there is one important difference: many of the components in a garden are of living material, which may not only increase in size but also undergo a change of character as they mature. To allow for this, a well-planned garden must have certain tolerances built into its concept, with longer-term plans as well as immediate solutions. For example, yew hedges will take

several years to grow but in the meantime you might erect a short-term boundary such as a fence.

You may decide to keep the garden as a single area, open and spacious in its appeal, or to divide it into two or more intimate and, perhaps, strikingly different garden "rooms." The way in which these areas are separated off from one another will provide one of the strongest structural elements of a garden. By building the internal divisions in the same material as the boundary structures, you will achieve unity or, from a new material, introduce contrast.

The plants you choose will of course reflect personal preference but they should always be suitable for the regional climate as well as the garden's orientation and type of soil; it is also important that they are an appropriate size for the scale of the garden. In some cases a single specimen of one plant may easily be sufficient, such as the ornamental rhubarb *(Rheum palmatum)*, but in other cases a clump or drift may be called for to give greater impact, such as a drift of bluebells through shrub planting, or anemones through a wood. A specimen tree or shrub, for example *Cornus controversa* 'Variegata,' or a herbaceous plant of dramatic shape like a

A pair of well-shaped yews, trimmed annually, flank the entrance from the garden to the terrace that runs along the front of a country house. The old stone flags echo the material used in the house walls, providing a sense of unity. In contrast to the sober dark green of the topiary, an urn on the terrace is planted with vibrantly colored summer bedding of petunias and pelargoniums.

globe artichoke *(Cynara scolymus)*, may become a feature in its own right, in the same way that a statue or a large container might be used, as a focal point within the garden. Such features can contribute greatly to the character and emphasis of the garden and should be carefully sited for maximum effect.

During the course of this book we look at the ingredients of a well-planned garden separately—from the vertical elements of boundary walls, fences and hedges and the horizontal elements of paths and paving, lawns and level changes, to the structural and ornamental features that furnish the garden and, of course, the plants that bring it to life by providing color and interest at different seasons. But it is only when the component parts of a garden are brought together as a cohesive whole that a garden really begins to work as a space which is well furnished, logical and attractive.

ABOVE *In this well-ordered garden a maturing walnut tree* (Juglans) *provides dappled shade for a broad expanse of lawn, in mid-summer an ideal location for* al fresco *eating. Rose-filled flower beds frame the lawn, linking house and garden. the flowers of Salvia sclarea turkestanica decorate the garden.*

LEFT *The formal layout of this garden "room" relies on strong structural components: box-edged corner beds and a central circular bed in an expanse of mellow herringbone brick paving. The opening in the enclosing beech hedge is flanked by yew cone-shaped sentinels.*

11

PLANNING THE GARDEN LAYOUT

What you require and expect from your garden has to be carefully balanced against what is appropriate, affordable and maintainable. Above all, when trying to decide just what a new garden should comprise, do bear in mind that this is your garden and it must be tailored primarily to your own requirements and to those of your family.

The well-planned garden does much to integrate the house with its plot. Here lavender-edged gravel paths take their proportions from features of the house façade and give all-weather access to the garden. Planting against the house walls helps to merge house and garden comfortably: Buddleia 'White Cloud' flanks the open door to the house, beneath which showy annuals of Cleome, Nicotiana and Cosmos give a rich summer display, edged with Alchemilla mollis. A wisteria clothes the gable end of the house with its rich green foliage. Pots for seasonal interest furnish the approach to the lawn.

13

Your own garden

A garden must be tailored to the needs of the family. Here an area of good planting comprising Helianthemum, Nepeta, Campanula, Alchemilla mollis, Spiraea arguta and lavender borders a sand-strewn area, part of which doubles as a child's sand box. This should be covered when not in use, to keep the sand clean.

The plan for your garden should take into account the individual needs of your family members, their different ages and interests and your general lifestyle—how much time you wish to spend gardening, whether the lawn needs to double as a play area, how often you might entertain in the garden. The length of time you intend to live in the house will influence certain decisions, as will the amount of money you are prepared to spend on it.

One of the most fundamental factors is the time that can be spent on the garden, whether it is purely your time or whether you plan to have some outside assistance. There is no point in having elaborate ideas and fanciful plans if they would be impossible to maintain within your own spare time, and prohibitively expensive if you were to employ skilled help. It is helpful to ascertain just how much time certain styles and sizes of garden will require. By visiting friends' gardens or those open to the public you can gain some idea of the upkeep involved in maintaining garden features such as shrub rose beds compared with herbaceous borders, a lawn compared with an expanse of gravel, or containers of annual plantings against summer-flowering shrubs. It is depressing to own a beautiful garden, only to discover that you cannot keep abreast of the weekly and monthly chores which the garden demands of you in order to look its best.

Drawing up your checklist

When deciding what, ideally, the garden should comprise, you might draw up a list of possibilities and the appropriate area in which to set them. Apart from the obvious elements that make up a garden—lawns, flower beds and a terrace—you should give some thought to the question of access, involving other hard surfaces such as paths and drives, and to siting essential features like sheds and compost bins.

An expanse of lawn is high on many people's list of priorities, particularly where a family with young children is concerned. A lawn also provides a good foreground for borders of plants. Another priority might be a paved area in a warm, sunny part of the garden, preferably near the house. Such a terrace would be more useful if it were given the protection and privacy of walls, hedges or trellis. Paths will be needed to link different areas of the garden and you may need to make, or improve, a drive.

Most gardens will need boundaries of some sort; particularly in an urban or suburban setting, a perimeter barrier is essential to close out neighbors, traffic and the world in general. You might also feel that divisions within the garden are a good idea, creating several individual garden areas within one plot, each with a distinctive character.

The number and the scale of beds and borders for mixed plantings should be appropriate to the size of the garden. Looking at the garden as a whole, you need to settle not only upon a style of planting, but also on a planting policy. Is the whole garden going to be planted for year-round color and interest, or for maximum impact around just one season? If the garden is divided into separate areas, should each one

Existing features can be successfully worked into a new garden layout. A broadly spreading tree (Catalpa bignonioides) provides welcome shade for an eating area. The tree links hard and soft surfaces while giving scale to this small garden.

This orderly vegetable plot is screened from the rest of the garden by yew hedges. The gravel paths are retained by "dog's tooth" edging bricks. Standard roses in the corners of the beds add a decorative feature, while a rustic screen supports climbers.

be given its own color theme and also a particular season? The garden planted for interest throughout the year can be said to have diluted appeal, with some plants flowering triumphantly while their close neighbors are only just emerging, and others fading and dying away. The seasonally planted garden or border, on the other hand, builds to a united, spectacular performance, peaking as one.

The inspiration for a garden can come from different sources; indeed the garden layout may combine several vignettes culled from admired gardens and perhaps reworked using modern materials. Favorite plants may be noted down from other gardens where their mature lines can be seen and appreciated at first hand. If you would also like beds to supply vegetables, fruit and cut flowers for the house, these can be as attractive as any other border provided they are planned well.

You may wish to consider the use of water in some form, be it a wall fountain, a small pond or a larger expanse of water. Water gives another dimension to a garden, opening up a range of different plants. Care must be taken with ponds where children are present; it would be safer to avoid water until they are older, but otherwise you could fit a rigid metal square mesh grill just beneath the surface, to be removed when the children have grown up.

Areas of a more utilitarian nature may be needed. A spot well away from the house should be found to site compost-making bins; you may also want an area to store manure or compost while it rots down. None of these should be in view from the house or the main part of the garden, and they may require some screening (see page 53). They should, however, be easily accessible, particularly for wheelbarrows or trailers. Close to the house but still obscured from view, areas for drying the washing and siting the trash cans need to be considered. Garden sheds, while a useful ingredient of a garden, should be positioned discreetly; they may be camouflaged by plants or with the use of trellis. The siting of a greenhouse needs care: while it should not be visible from the house, it must be in full sun.

Assessing your plot

ABOVE *A garden may contain several different sets of growing conditions. Here* Dianthus *thrives in the freely draining soil in the top of a low stone retaining wall.*

RIGHT *Even a small front garden should have a planned layout. This design has circular paving of imitation granite blocks, with newly planted corner beds. A Victorian chimney pot and rope-twist edging stones link with the period of the house.*

The potential, and the limitations, of your site have to be considered on several different levels—and preferably simultaneously. There are certain things you cannot change, such as the shape of the plot and the type of climate, but it is through working with what you have and contributing your own ideas that you will achieve a garden of unique character. We may divide the considerations into roughly two categories: those relating to the plot's shape, size and general layout, and the influences that climate, soil and orientation will have on what you can plant.

Considerations of shape and size

The overall shape of the plot should not necessarily dictate the layout of your garden, for any short-comings can be disguised by numerous visual tricks. Dense plantings of shrubs will camouflage the regular perimeter lines. Internal divisions of hedges, trellis or walls can be used to mislead the eye. A long, narrow plot will be foreshortened by the use of a division near the house with a view through to the remaining garden; conversely a short plot could be visually lengthened by placing a division at the far end of the garden, half-concealing a small area at the extremity of the plot. Always avoid a path running through the middle of a long, narrow garden, which would only accentuate its linear proportions. By using different-shaped trees and shrubs, a short garden may be made to appear considerably longer than it is. Broadly rounded trees and shrubs such as *Viburnum opulus* 'Roseum,' planted near the house, or the beginning of the view, should be followed by decreasingly smaller shrubs with a slimmer outline. Features such as a series of arches can also be intentionally reduced in size away from the house visually to elongate the garden.

A garden dominated by a house in the middle of the plot will need to be planned and planted to maximize the space. The best solution is to have flower borders on the boundaries, and fill them with small-leaved, fine-textured foliage plants, restrained in growth, keeping the area around the building as free and spacious as possible.

Color can play a significant part in enhancing perspective. If bright, strong colors are used close to the beginning of the view, along with dark-leaved plants and white flowers, running away to pale pinks and blues with pale or silver foliage, a great sense of distance will be achieved. Conversely, if a white-flowered shrub or a white-painted bench is placed at the end of a garden it will appear to jump out, shattering the pleasing impression of distance created.

The general layout

The starting point for the garden's layout and materials should come from the house. It is best to let the period of the house influence the overall style of the garden, by using details and materials which relate back to the house. This is not to say that a traditional house built in the 1940s cannot have a cottage-style garden looking back to the nineteenth century, or a more contemporary style of garden, using areas of gravel and raised beds. From the proportions and façade of a house you will still find inspiration for lines of paths, the position of a gateway and the proportions of a border. The brick or stone from which the house is built can also be echoed in terracing and walling materials. The well-planned garden should help to merge a house into its immediate surroundings, giving the impression that the house has grown up out of the garden.

When considering your plot, it is easy to look only as far as your own boundaries and perimeter walls, and not at the houses and gardens of your neighbors. But these may, now or in the future, have a significant influence on your own garden. Over-sized trees near a boundary can cause severe shade problems, as can a tall evergreen boundary hedge which has developed into a row of conifer trees; these will also create drought conditions in their vicinity. High windows in neighboring houses are difficult to screen. Using evergreens for screening may inadvertently draw the eye to the offending building, particularly in a garden containing few other evergreens, whereas a deciduous and evergreen mixture will soften and greatly reduce the impact of nearby

buildings. Alternatively you could use plant-clad trellis to screen something unsightly or to block a view (see page 53).

Occasionally it happens that structures on adjacent land, rather than being hidden or screened, can be "borrowed" as a feature for your own garden. A handsome specimen tree, a distant church tower, or a fine view may be used as a focal point; this will extend the horizons of a small garden in particular. In such cases your own plantings should direct the eye to what is beyond.

The climate

Factors such as regional and local climate, the type of soil and the orientation of the site will strongly affect what you plant in your garden, and they are all closely interrelated. A regional climate is influenced by the region's relative latitude and position within a

Where appropriate, the materials from which a house is built should be echoed in those chosen for the garden. The architecture of this highly decorative house has been extended to the white-painted boundary fence, in the elaborately detailed shaping of the pickets.

landmass. The prevailing atmospheric conditions create a general pattern of regional weather which includes factors such as the average amount of seasonal rainfall, the degree of frost during winter and the highest temperatures reached in summer. Within a localized area the weather trends may differ somewhat from the regional climate as a result of land contours and areas of vegetation such as woodland; in cities the density of buildings often creates a more sheltered environment but the level of pollution may restrict what you can grow.

A microclimate is a pocket of unique atmospheric conditions prevailing in a garden or garden area. The effect of a high enclosing wall, a protective hedge or a clump of trees would be to reduce the wind in a part of the garden and, in the case of the wall, to reflect or store the sun's heat. An overhanging canopy of trees with a pond below will give a sheltered, moist atmosphere in its vicinity. A hot, sunny corner created by two walls will greatly mitigate the possibly unfavorable conditions of a regional and local climate, permitting you to grow less hardy plants than could be grown in an exposed neighboring garden.

Cold winds in late winter can cause as much damage as the most severe midwinter temperatures, so in any open, exposed garden it is advisable to create a protective barrier to reduce the wind speed. In areas subject to heavy falls of snow you should avoid having tiered evergreen plants, as a weight of snow will be liable to tear the branches off. To live in a particularly dry or an exceptionally wet area should be met as a challenge. Either climatic extreme will disqualify you from growing certain plants, but provided you select species suited to the prevailing conditions, then they will of course thrive.

The type of soil

When assessing the type of soil in a garden it is usual to talk of its chemical type as well as its texture and structure. Soils may be chemically defined on a pH scale of one to ten, to show whether they are predominantly alkaline (lime-containing) or acid (lime-free); a soil is said to be neutral at pH 7. It is important to discover which type of soil you have as there are plant groups associated specifically with

each, as well as a wide choice of plants which will tolerate either tendency. Your soil may easily be tested by using a simple home tester kit; it will be given a pH reading (percent hydrogen in concentration). The lower the reading, the greater the acidity; the higher the reading, the more alkaline the soil is. Plants such as *Rhododendron*, *Gaultheria*, *Kalmia* and *Pieris* all require lime-free acid soils, whereas *Iris pallida*, *Helleborus orientalis*, *Pulsatilla* and *Centranthus* thrive on highly alkaline soils.

The texture of a soil is judged by the size of its particles: sandy soils are made up of large particles whereas in clay soils fine particles are predominant. In between these two extremes are loams, which comprise a mixture of the two. A heavy soil is one whose fine soil particles are tightly bound together by a film of water occupying the spaces between the particles, making it heavy to dig. Heavy soils might encompass clays, clay loams and the finest silts. A light soil comprises large particles, the spaces between them being too big to be held together by water tension. The lighter soil is therefore more open, resulting in a sandy or a sandy loam tendency.

The structure of a soil refers to the way the particles are held together, in crumbs or clods. The size of these dictates the nature of the soil structure to a great extent. If they are very small, the vital air pores will be largely absent from the soil; if too large, the air pores will be too widely distributed to be beneficial to young root growth. Unlike the texture of a soil, we can at least influence its structure by adding organic material which will assist the formation of crumbs. This process is also encouraged by natural weathering agents such as frost, rain and sun.

Organic matter can be added to soils in the form of farmyard manure, garden compost or bark chippings. These condition the soil, adding bulk and improving its nutrient- and moisture-holding capacity; they also add nutrients, but only to a limited extent. To a light sandy or stony soil the organic matter gives substance, and helps to keep its structure open and fresh, whereas it lightens a heavy soil.

The orientation

The orientation of house and garden forms a subtle partnership with the climate, their interplay dictat-

The strong lines on which this garden's semi-formal layout is based ensure that it looks good all year round. The well-furnished garden "areas" relate easily one to another and the garden as a whole has a sense of unity. From the hub of the garden, with its focal point of the sundial placed on a graveled circle, paths, vistas and border designs take their reference. Box-edged geometric beds radiate out from the graveled circle, while yew hedges form internal divisions. An elaborately shaped pair of yew piers, trained on frames, end the first hedge and more topiary in pots furnishes a seating area on the right. Trees planted on the boundaries contribute to the garden's tranquility and screen neighboring buildings.

ing the choice of successful plants. Whether the garden faces north, south, east or west will determine the levels of light and warmth or the degree of prolonged cold and shade and at what time the sunlight will pass over certain areas of the garden. The layout of the garden should be arranged to take advantage of the range of conditions within it—for example, siting a terrace to catch the evening sun. Plants should also be selected to suit the diverse range of microclimates created by differing orientations: cool areas of deep shade and moisture will provide fine habitats for hardy ferns, hostas and pulmonarias, whereas those plants requiring warmth will revel in the heat and direct light of an area facing or tilting into the sun.

Style and planting

The style of planting, and how this is integrated with the basic structure, will greatly influence the character of the garden. Where a garden is divided into distinct areas, isolated from one another, several different styles may be adopted. It is too simplistic to consider adopting the obvious extremes of formal and informal; however, a blended composition of the two in varying strengths of each will provide noticeable changes of character. Clipped evergreen hedges and geometric evergreen shapes, combined with straight-sided, square-cornered flower borders edged with dwarf hedges, would be purely formal. But if this rigid framework is combined with a lush, flowery planting of herbaceous perennials and annuals, the integration of the two styles can be remarkable. Conversely, an informal lawn with spreading trees and shrubs underplanted with naturalized bulbs among billowing old-fashioned roses may be greatly enhanced by the presence of some formal, clipped evergreen shapes.

The way in which a garden is maintained will also dramatically alter its general appearance. A rigorously pruned and trimmed garden, with hedges angularly cut and shrubs kept to modest proportions, will give a totally different impression from one in which hedges are permitted to broaden and waver slightly off-course, and shrubs are left to make natural billowing shapes, even if the selection of plants in them is more or less identical.

Measuring the site

Many gardeners will consider a structural plan unnecessary, preferring to use a bundle of canes, a ball of thick, visible string and a hosepipe to physically "create" the layout of their new garden. However, this course of action makes it difficult to envisage the site without many of its existing features, leading to a tendency to build the new layout on the bones of the present garden. It is also difficult to lay out several alternative proposals on the same site without causing confusion. Putting a garden plan on paper provides the ideal point of reference—it allows time for a considered choice, while enabling different ideas to be superimposed upon a basic outline plan.

Before drawing up a plan, decide what areas are to be included. Take in the whole plot if it is a relatively small garden. But if it is larger, with areas that can easily be divided off and taken as single entities, draw a series of plans that relate to each other to show details, and also draw a small-scale plan of the whole garden.

Before taking any measurements of the existing garden, draw a rough sketch of it, marking on one side of the house, plus any boundary lines, paths and terraces, the shapes of any flower borders, the shape of a lawn, and any specimen trees or other strong features that exist. Draw this out on a large sheet of paper, preferably fixed to a board, to facilitate writing on it "in the field." On a smaller sheet measurements have to be squeezed in and can all too easily become confused.

Now go out into the garden, having equipped yourself with two tape measures, one of them preferably a long surveyor's tape (these can be rented). You should ideally have someone with you, to hold one end of the tape. When measuring on your own, push a fine steel rod through the ring on the end of the tape and then push the rod into the ground, to hold the tape firmly in place. After taking each measurement, stop and write the dimensions on the sketch plan; if many measurements converge in one area, it may be helpful to mark on fine arrows to relate each measurement to its line.

What goes on the plan

In the majority of cases a plan of the garden will include at least one side of the house and it is a good idea to begin measuring here. Take the overall dimensions, then measure the individual sections of wall which make up that façade, with windows and doors accurately measured and indicated. From these points the layout of the garden will develop: paths

Plotting existing features

To measure irregular shapes, curves and "floating features," fix the longer tape to an obvious point, such as one side of a house window or a post on the boundary fence, and extend it out at 90 degrees by measuring a 3:4:5 triangle as shown on the right. Indicate this line of the tape on your sketch plan. Using the shorter tape, and taking a secondary 3:4:5 triangle from your orientation line, measure out to the feature in question. To plot a curve, measure out every couple of yards from the long orientation line.

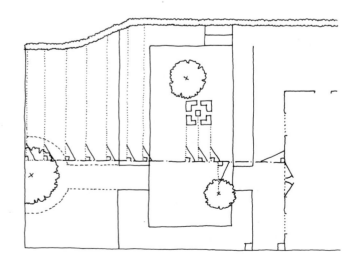

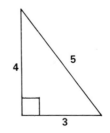

The most accurate way of judging a right angle is to measure out a triangle with the sides in the ratio 3:4:5.

The proximity of house and garden on this relatively small plot is mitigated by the presence of the huge linden tree. By softening the angles made with the house, a softer, more inward-looking garden is created. The planting below the tree would need generous feeding and mulching to compensate for being robbed of many nutrients by the tree's roots. The gravel path between house and garden serves as an outdoor seating area; its direct access to the broad lawn is broken only by the planting of standard roses (Rosa 'The Fairy'). A main path runs off at right angles to the house, while side paths enclose a grid of low box-edged beds. The boundary walls are reduced in impact by the use of wall shrubs and climbers, including a productive fig tree which takes advantage of a warm, sheltered angle between two walls.

and terraces running off from windows and door-ways, walls and hedges leading from the corners of the building. Now measure and mark on all the boundaries of the garden, or garden area, jotting down whether it is a wall, fence or hedge and from what material it is made. An indication of the height of each boundary is also useful.

Any existing paths or terraces should be measured next. Straight and parallel borders, paths or retaining walls can easily be marked, using measurements taken from the boundaries. Curved lines and edges are more difficult to indicate, and for these you will need both tape measures (see opposite). The same applies to what might be called "floating features," which include trees, island beds, a summer house or a pond which are not attached or linked to their surroundings in any way, often being positioned in an expanse of lawn. To measure distant features, the line of the long tape measure may be extended by the use of poles, canes or surveyor's ranging rods.

As this is not a planting plan, all that is required at this stage is to indicate on your site plan any areas

of existing shrubs and trees and perhaps whether they are deciduous or evergreen. It is useful to show the diameter of a tree's canopy, to remind you to allow for shade in that vicinity. Any retaining walls with changes of level should be shown, with a note to the effect that there is a level change; a bank of grass leading to a level change should also be indicated at its lower and upper height. If you know where electric cables, water pipes and waste pipes run, it is important to include this information on your plan.

If you have not already done so, and as a final check, measure the overall width and length of the plot in one go, at both ends and through the middle. It is dangerous to depend on adding up composite measurements to give a total length. Take into account any slopes, which would add slightly to your total measurements. A good test for accuracy is to draw out your longer tape measure, fixing it diagonally across the whole plot and measuring the length; then do the same between the opposite two corners. When the final drawing is made, check this distance on the plan to verify your accuracy.

Drawing up the plan

Putting the plan on paper

Draw this initial plan on graph paper and to scale, using thick lines for the garden's boundaries and any existing features which you intend to keep. You may then superimpose new ideas, indicating broad areas of planting, open areas of lawn and basic hard surfaces. Features which will probably be redundant in the new layout should be drawn using a thin line; look at these in the context of your new ideas to see whether they can be reworked into the new plan.

1 *Lawn*
2 *Proposed utility area*
3 *Proposed orchard*
4 *Shed*
5 *Shrub planting*
6 *Gravel path*
7 *Herbaceous perennials and shrubs*
8 *Sundial*
9 *Rose beds*
10 *Terrace*
11 *Fence*
12 *Hedge*

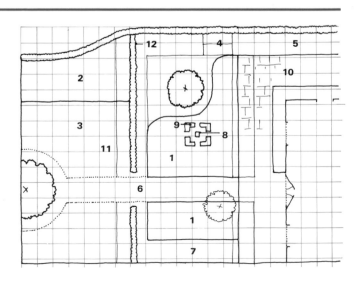

A change of level in the garden can be dealt with in several ways (see pages 86–91). Here a shallow flight of steps cleverly links two soft lawn areas, the broad banks on either side being treated as lushly planted borders filled with philadelphus, centranthus, hellebores, hostas, astrantias and pulmonarias. The box edging to the borders on either side of the steps mimics the outline of the risers, while a dividing yew hedge, ending in architecturally shaped piers, backs the borders at the higher level. The opening in the hedge and the flight of steps themselves lead the eye to a centrally placed specimen tree in the adjacent garden area.

Having gathered all the information relating to your site, you can decide what form the plan will take. Unless you have access to a drawing board, the easiest solution is to use squared graph paper. Whether you are making a plan on graph paper or using scale rules, the most important consideration is to draw the plan big enough, using an appropriate scale. Use large sheets of graph paper and experiment to find what size of square will represent a square yard, while enabling the whole plan to fit on the sheet. There is nothing worse than trying to draw details that are no bigger than a postage stamp. I generally use a scale of 1:100 for general structure plans and 1:50 for more detailed planting plans.

Using an HB pencil, I mark out the boundaries of the garden first, centralizing the drawing as far as possible and making the most of the sheet of paper. If the house features in the drawing, draw this in next, indicating the doors and windows; write in the heights of the windowsills from ground level, to enable a specific choice of plant heights beneath the windows. Once all the walls, hedges and buildings are in place, the adjoining features may be plotted in relation to these: the paths, terraces, retaining walls, level changes and any internal divisions such as walls, hedges and fences, against which existing borders may be drawn. Finally, mark onto the plan any "floating features" such as trees or island beds.

This plan will now contain all the useful information gathered from the site; it should be checked against the measurement of the original diagonal tie lines and, if correct, inked over to make it permanent. If you draw on tracing paper over the graph paper, mistakes in permanent ink can easily be removed with a utility-knife blade, and copies can be printed from it with ease and clarity. Use a fine-nibbed pen for the small internal details which may be ignored in the new scheme, and a broad-nibbed pen to emphasize fixed features such as house walls and boundaries, internal divisions, paths and terracing, and the lines of borders or lawn areas that you intend to keep. Trees and spreading shrubs should have their center point marked with a cross, and

their outer canopy line ringed with a series of short, faint dashes. Add an arrow point to indicate north, with a note of the scale used. Once the structure plan of existing features is complete, you should make several copies of it, safeguarding the original.

Producing a new garden plan

You can work on your copies to produce a variety of different options for the garden layout, and at this stage it is worth keeping an open mind and considering all manner of possibilities. You may decide to base the garden very much on existing lines and features or totally to abandon what is there and begin afresh. A newly built house may have a garden consisting only of boundaries, so here a creative mind and a strong imagination will be needed.

This is the time to call to mind all that you would want your garden to provide (see page 14), and the plants you particularly like, set against the amount of time you will be able to spare to look after it. Remember that the aspect and climate will greatly influence the plants and materials used (see page 18). You will need to consider the character and period of the house and its surroundings and what you can afford financially. Your plans should also reflect how long you intend to live in this particular house, which will to some extent determine the type of plantings you choose for the garden.

You can draw up a number of plans containing different proposals, but do not necessarily look at them in isolation; points from each may be brought together to form a strong structure, combining a greater number of your priorities. Make sure you allocate enough time to this stage, mulling over the various combinations, looking out of windows to envisage how different ideas would look from strategic positions. Eventually a general plan will emerge, no doubt with some compromises but hopefully with many of your requirements intact. It is important to have considered the area as a whole, with thought to the long-term appeal of the garden, even if this will take several years of phased construction and planting.

Putting the plan into action

Once the chosen scheme has been "inked in" on the original plan, more copies can be taken from this, on which priorities of work can be identified and time schedules allocated. Whether we are talking about a plot the size of several fields, that of a tennis court, or a few square yards, it is all too easy to spend a lot of money on designing, remodeling and planting a garden. But once you have decided on an overall scheme, individual tasks and projects may be put into action as and when time and money permit, spreading the workload and the expenditure.

By building a garden over several years, but in a logical series of stages, a greater pleasure is derived from seeing it take shape than from it arriving like a fitted kitchen to be assembled in a matter of days. You also ensure that any money spent goes on plants or materials that are *needed*, and avoid the annual dash to the garden center in late spring to buy plants to brighten up the garden for another season — possibly only to discover these to be wholly unsuitable in years to come. To carry out at least some of the work yourself will give greater satisfaction than a grand scheme undertaken on your behalf by a builder or landscape gardener.

Developing a garden in stages also gives a staggered introduction to the maintenance required of it. This can prove useful, and you may decide during the garden's subsequent development to reduce high-maintenance, complex areas, detailed in their composition, and replace them with simpler ideas, often with equal effect. The stages can be indicated on your plan by the use of different color shadings.

Trying out the layout

Before even embarking on the first stage of the work, it will prove useful to mark out many of the intended features on the site. Bamboo canes laid end to end give a visual impression of the outline of a border, and short sections of bamboo canes knocked into the ground like pegs, with light-colored twine fastened between them, enable corners, curves and lines to be suggested. Hedge lines, walls, terraces and steps can all be shown in this way and if some of the areas do not feel right, there is nothing lost by changing your mind at this preliminary stage. The sweeping curve of a lawn or drive may be portrayed by a supple hose and a formal line of clipped topiary shapes by upturned trash cans. Single specimen trees positioned across a more distant lawn can be represented by sturdy tree stakes painted white, enabling you to view them from all angles and distances. The spacing of medium-sized to large trees is particularly difficult. One can never imagine that two "poles" sited 50 ft. apart will one day touch branches.

COLOR KEY FOR THE PLAN

■ **Stage one**

■ **Stage two**

□ **Stage three**

■ **Longer-term**

The order of work

Stage one Priority should be given to those areas nearest the house that affect everyday life, such as drives, paths and terraces. Defining the garden boundaries is another priority, particularly where privacy is lacking. Remember that walls and fences are expensive but they create the desired effect instantly, whereas hedges, trees and shrubs are considerably cheaper but "expensive" in the

length of time they take to achieve their purpose, so it is advisable to establish any long-term plantings, such as hedges, in the first year. Since in this first phase the watering of young trees, shrubs and hedging plants will be all-important, it is wise to connect up at least one outside tap, from which a hose can be run. Space for a compost heap, if practical, must also be found at this early stage.

The remaining ground needs to be cleared of undergrowth and general neglect, removing any unwanted garden features, such as trees or old pergolas, unless they have a purpose in the short term. For example, an old hedge or line of trees may give temporary shelter to better placed but vulnerable young plants for the first two years, and a garden shed could usefully be kept until it is in the way. Old materials such as good

stone, bricks and edging tiles that are taken up may be cleaned of cement and stacked for re-use in another form, since such materials are expensive to buy in quantity.

Weeds, particularly perennial species, must be eradicated by the careful use of appropriate herbicides or frequent cultivation, by deep digging, forking or hoeing. Where plant borders are to be established, the soil should be improved,

incorporating well-rotted organic matter to give a better texture and condition, and organic fertilizer to improve the soil's fertility. If there is only a thin layer of topsoil present, overlying subsoil, you should consider adding extra soil now, or indeed total re-soiling — that is, removing and storing the sparse topsoil, digging out a layer of subsoil for disposal, and bringing in extra topsoil to combine with the little removed.

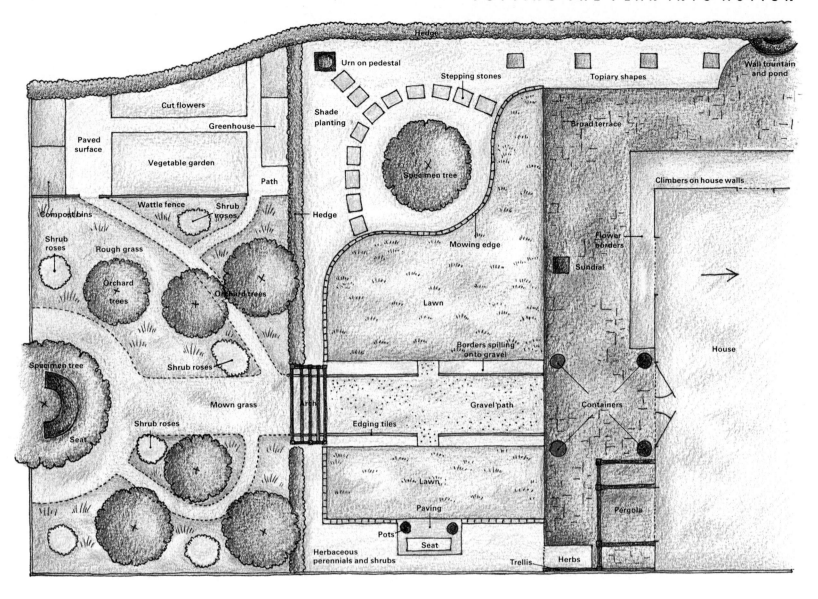

Hedge

Urn on pedestal

Stepping stones

Topiary shapes

Wall fountain and pond

Cut flowers

Shade planting

Greenhouse

Broad terrace

Paved surface

Vegetable garden

Climbers on house walls

Path

Compost bins

Wattle fence

Shrub roses

Hedge

Flower borders

Shrub roses

Rough grass

Sundial

Specimen tree

Mowing edge

Orchard trees

Lawn

House

Orchard trees

Shrub roses

Specimen tree

Borders spilling onto gravel

Mown grass

Arch

Gravel path

Containers

Edging tiles

Seat

Shrub roses

Lawn

Paving

Pergola

Pots

Seat

Herbaceous perennials and shrubs

Trellis

Herbs

Any other earthworks should be undertaken at this stage, including drainage of the site, the laying of water mains for garden taps and electric cables for the eventual provision of light and power to certain areas of the garden. A flight of steps may require illumination, and a power point in the heart of the garden will reduce the length of extension cable necessary for trimming hedges or mowing the lawn.

To give yourself some encouragement in the first year, when perhaps there is little color in the garden, plant up some large pots or tubs close to the house, which you can enjoy even while the rest of the garden is in a state of disorganization.

Stage two The second phase of a staged plan may be given over to large internal projects such as constructing paths and retaining walls. Areas to be treated as

lawn should be established now, on cleared ground, and roses may be ordered and planted as it will take at least two years before they begin to develop their true character. Dividing walls or fences should be erected.

Stage three A third phase may involve the establishment of a herbaceous border as well as a vegetable plot if these form part of the plan. Culinary herbs

grown in containers may now be sited in a sunny border near the kitchen. Climbing plants against house walls can be planted as soon as possible but if building work on the house is still in progress, this may mean waiting until later. You may at this stage contemplate some improvements to what is already in place, for example the laying of a mowing edge against plant-filled borders, or stepping stones across a lawn for access.

Longer-term Once the basic layout and key features are in place, further embellishments may be carried out as and when time and money permit. Solidly built pergolas or arches could replace homemade rustic ones. Areas originally surfaced inexpensively with gravel might eventually be paved with stone or brick, using the well-firmed base already in place. Garden furniture and pots and urns may be chosen and sited.

THE VERTICAL DIMENSION

Vertical elements in the garden may range from a solid boundary wall or dividing hedge to a semi-open wooden picket fence or trelliswork screen, or may simply comprise a well-placed tree or group of shrubs. Whether made of living or man-made materials, they all play a part not only in defining and dividing up the plot, but in contributing to the whole character and ambience of the garden.

Enclosing a small garden area with high walls creates a space rich in sensory delights by trapping scents on the calm air and amplifying small sounds. Mellow brick and old stone walls are clothed with bowers of climbing roses and scented Philadelphus microphyllus, to create a fine display in early summer.

Why create verticals?

FAR RIGHT *This secluded garden is framed by boundary fences, softened on the right by a profusion of climbing roses. The archway divides off another garden "room."*

BELOW *This striking arch, with the large, rose-mauve flowers of a* Clematis *'Nelly Moser' and the double pink blooms of the climbing shrub rose,* Rosa *'Constance Spry,' creates a natural-looking division and provides a glimpse of the rest of the garden beyond.*

When confronted with a pleasant, flat, open site, why do we immediately try to find ways of camouflaging it, covering it with visual obstructions or making it appear larger (or smaller) than it really is? Many of the reasons are probably more psychological than practical. To own a plot of land around your house which has no vertical boundary markers, leaving the house to stand free of physical barriers, makes the property appear vulnerable. The finest of houses with the most glorious of views will still give a sense of unease if it is wide open to the surrounding countryside. Boundary enclosures give a reassuring, protective embrace around the house, marking the territory which accompanies it. Equally, a cottage or suburban house, with a modest garden of intimate confines, will benefit from further protective enclosures to give privacy from neighbors and from roads.

While this may explain why outer boundaries are erected, it does not make clear the reasons why we clutter the center of the garden with visual blocks. It is often, and I believe rightly, said that when standing with your back to the house you should not be able to view the whole garden. There should be areas, however small, which are hidden away, demanding to be investigated. A short section of hedge with an arch set within it, protruding from a boundary hedge, will be enough to tempt people off the terrace and farther into the garden. By creating a little of the unknown, by stopping the eye short of the boundary, a degree of mystery is introduced. You have also brought movement into the garden by compelling people to walk through it, which in turn may lead them to other areas still to be discovered.

Many garden sites are flat, without a single contour. To give variety and interest to an otherwise bland site, the levels can be raised and lowered by using blocks of shrubs, low hedges and dwarf walls. Where higher vertical obstructions are used to form boundaries or internal divisions, the installation of familiar features such as hedges, fences and trees makes the garden a more comfortable place to be in. A small area hemmed in with high divisions of walls or hedges brings you into close contact with plants at head height, the proximity trapping and concentrating any strong scents. Sounds are also altered, amplifying some, deadening others which, combined with the different scents, helps to create that most elusive of qualities, atmosphere. Simple blocks of evergreen or deciduous trees and shrubs will bring the essential quality of light and shade to a plot, both in themselves and in the shadows they create across a lawn or within a border.

The style and material from which a wall, fence or hedge is constructed will greatly add to—or detract from—the garden as a whole. It is therefore important that the overriding theme or period of the garden is reflected in some aspect of this vertical dimension. On a more practical note, the vertical element plays a major role in the use and selection of climbing plants for the garden. Walls and fences may become hedge-like in just a few years, sporting fine flowering climbers on every aspect of the garden.

Divisions and focal points

The phrase "vertical dimension" is a rather sterile but all-embracing term for a wide range of animate and inanimate garden structures, many of great beauty. The dimension includes the categories of hard and soft landscaping, living materials as well as man-made and natural ones, and both solid structures and more open or see-through ones.

Rigid lines may be created by the use of brick or stone walls; some hedges have a similar appearance to walls while others create soft lines in sympathy with other plantings. A fence gives a solid, but thin and light impression in a garden, but a see-through trellis will be lighter still and may be partially camouflaged with climbing plants. Iron railings denote a garden division or boundary often so subtle that from a distance they prove invisible, which is ideal where fine views or good architecture are concerned and should not be obscured.

Pergolas and arches may, and should, be delicate-looking structures, whether they are free-standing or fixed to a garden wall or building. They are useful devices for merging heavy, dense walls into the garden, acting as a transitional structure from the solid to the soft, especially if they are clad with twining and climbing plants.

Small buildings such as a summer house, a gazebo, a pavilion or even just a bower can temper a very natural-looking garden, reassuring the visitor that civilization has touched here. They usually have some architectural merit in themselves and also help to give a human scale to the garden. More is written about these buildings in the chapter on structural features, page 93.

Last and what, quite conceivably, should have been first, there are trees and shrubs which, between them, will probably account for more vertical diversions than all the other categories put together. For creating an informal barrier or a statuesque focal point, a natural-looking screening or a formal evergreen shape, there is little to compare with well-selected plant material.

Establishing boundaries

Where a boundary requires only a definition, without the need for privacy or protection, an open structure may be used. These cast-iron railings make the perfect airy boundary for a town garden, at the back of a border comprising roses, campanulas, delphiniums, hardy geraniums and variegated lemon balm. The open railings also take advantage of taller shrubs in the neighboring garden, including red-leaved Acer palmatum, *golden privet and a camellia.*

When deciding upon a form of garden boundary, it is important to recognize what you are shutting the garden off from, and act accordingly. It may be neighbors or animals—from the next-door cat or dog to perhaps sheep or cattle from neighboring farmland. Traffic noise, or the sounds emanating from a neighbor's swimming pool, may be baffled by the use of good boundary hedging. Strong winds may be reduced in their ferocity by planting windbreak trees and hedges or the use of certain forms of fencing and trellis. Some boundaries may create problems rather than solving them. A solid wall or even a dense, evergreen hedge may trap cold, freezing air if placed along the base of a hill, creating a frost trap or pocket where frost lingers all day. A more open structure will permit the cold air to roll on down and out of the garden.

What height?

Whatever material is used, the height of the boundary is something you must decide at the beginning. Remember that the higher the barrier, the greater the area of shade cast by it, especially in winter. Where you can establish a link between the height of an existing structure and that of your boundary, this will create a happy flow of levels—between, for example, the garage or outhouse roof and a fence, or between a section of wall and a hedge. Where an existing feature is too high or too low to match, a harmonious link may still be possible by starting your boundary structure at a corresponding height before swooping it up or down in an arc to the preferred height.

Providing privacy may be of paramount importance but a boundary screen that is oversized for the garden as a whole can be a high price to pay. When the height exceeds 8 ft., there is the danger of a loss of proportion and in many modest gardens a boundary 6½ ft. tall will be quite high enough. Instead of creating a massive single screen, it is better to target your screening devices at specific undesirable spots. In front of your boundary fence, wall or hedge you might plant a clump of trees to blot out an offending view which demands greater height in just one place along a stretch of boundary. Where extremely high walls, fences or trellis are essential, their hard, angular appearance may be minimized by the use of a mixture of climbers to give a lush, verdant covering. A garden enclosed by high hedges may be softened in line and form by planting, for example, beds of shrub roses at their foot, obscuring the hard angle between ground and hedge.

How dense?

Large or solid boundaries are not always necessary or desirable. Often, all that is required of a boundary is a demarcation line to differentiate private property from public land. In such cases, a low or semi-open structure will be sufficient. This might take the form of a wooden picket fence or an elegant iron railing, a low or dwarf stone wall or a hedge of box *(Buxus sempervirens)*. In an exposed situation a light, open structure such as a picket fence, which will filter and break the force of a strong prevailing wind, may be preferable to a solid structure such as a woven-panel fence. A deciduous hedge of hawthorn *(Crataegus)* will reduce the strength of the wind by filtering, whereas a dense yew hedge would only divert it.

High protective boundary walls are often desirable in areas of open countryside where strong winds and security need to be considered. Though the benefit of wind protection will be felt over a relatively short distance, it provides a good climbing surface for delicate plants needing shelter such as this Escallonia. The simple slatted gate forms an opening within an internal dividing hedge of Lonicera nitida, *offering an enticing glimpse of the grassy walk over which plants spill from both sides; these include* Alchemilla mollis, Hemerocallis, Geranium *'Claridge Druce' and G. 'Wargrave Pink.'*

The materials

When new materials are to be used to construct the boundaries, study the existing features of the property first, to see what can be learned from them. Look around the locality to see the traditional materials used. You may find ideas for a particular color of brick, its coursing and pattern when used in walling, as well as the type of coping used with it; you might decide on the mixture to use in a mixed-genus hedge to mimic the natural farmland hedges, or you may get inspiration for the style of fence from that used locally and the material from which it has been created. To attempt to "tie in" with a local material or with a particular detail from the house gives the garden a touch of individuality, preventing it from looking like the standard garden put together from the builders' yard and garden center.

Remember that a boundary does not simply have to serve its utilitarian purpose; it can also amuse and delight. Fences could be surmounted by trellis tops dripping with flowers; the supporting posts can have ball finials of wood or even clipped ivy. Hedges may have fanciful castellations or more finials clipped out of their tops, or even protruding buttresses that seemingly prevent their sides from falling. Ironwork railings can be formal period re-creations, but they can just as easily be flowing futuristic designs. Some brick walls are built with geometric patterns using bricks of contrasting color, others incorporate panels into which a trained fan or espaliered fruit tree may be grown. Do not let your imagination stop at the point where you must have a wall here or a hedge there, but think hard about how you will develop the design of that boundary structure.

Internal divisions

The precisely clipped yew hedge ending in taller "piers" creates a living division. The wrought-iron gate allows views of the sheltered garden beyond, where Carpenteria californica *and* Vitis coignetiae *thrive. The sun-loving plants sprawling on to the stone path include* Lavandula *and* Kniphofia.

shrubs. Formal divisions convey a strong architectural influence upon a garden. Where a softer, less defined impression is sought, a semi-open structure of trellis and climbing plants may be used, allowing glimpses of the next compartment. Generally speaking, the smaller the area to be enclosed, the less appropriate a very high dividing structure becomes. It is difficult to give an ideal height for an internal division, but when 7 ft. is exceeded, great care must be taken with the choice of material, or the structure may become overpowering and heavy.

Even in a garden comprising just two separate areas, a bland, predictable scene will be transformed into two remarkably different plots. With a large enough opening, the garden beyond may be sighted, but not revealed, from the house and upon entering it there will be a distinct sense of leaving the house and its environment behind. If the areas concerned are not large, then deciduous hedges of hornbeam or beech, or a section of trellis, may be used to divide them, allowing more light into the garden during the dark days of winter. On an exposed site, further divisions within the garden will give extra protection against the wind. Warm, sunny backdrops to plants will be created, but it is important to remember that behind such a generally ideal aspect there is a cold position which will remain damp and shady on days when its favorable counterpart will be the reverse.

Creating garden rooms provides for a greater range of planting possibilities and themes. Color will define the mood of a garden like no other. A pale theme, using a combination of white (*Spirea arguta*), cream *Rosa* 'Nevada,' and pale pink *Kolkwitzia amabilis*, would shine out, even in the half light of evening, in a space enclosed by evergreen hedges of yew or laurel.

Another theme could be one of scent, for the confines of a small enclosure help to trap the still air upon which many of the delicate scents travel. A scented hedge such as *Osmanthus delavayi* could form the "walls" or fencing or trellis may be used to support sweet-smelling honeysuckle (*Lonicera periclymenum*) or summer jasmine (*Jasminum officinale*).

Garden divisions may be a practical necessity, to separate off or reduce the visual impact of a utilitarian area of the garden (see Screening, pages 53–5), or they may take on a purely aesthetic role.

To subdivide a garden plot into a series of themed compartments is a popular idea inspired in this century by the famous English gardens of Hidcote Manor and Sissinghurst Castle, where large gardens are turned into a series of interconnecting outside "rooms." These rooms are formed by solid walls or hedging, but could equally be created with the use of fences or trellis, or dense plantings of informal

Garden walls

All walling materials fall into one of three basic types: brick, stone and concrete. Within these categories, strong distinctions are usually caused by the use of locally available materials. The color and texture of both brick and stone will vary according to their origin and to the way they have been dressed or manufactured. Concrete can vary in color and texture if one of its components, aggregate, is partially exposed while it is damp, revealing a distinctive local material.

The size of the component bricks, stones or concrete pieces and the way in which they are assembled are as important as the material itself. In a high, long wall the components used may be significantly larger than in a short, low wall where the use of small courses is preferable. Where possible it is a good idea to use local materials and to echo one of those found in the site. When it is not practical or financially possible to use an identical material, then a similar alternative or artificial reconstituted material of the correct color and approximate texture should be found.

Across the regions, stone ranges in color from cream through browns to reds and yellows, and bricks from palest cream through pinks and reds to blue. Whereas bricks will vary only slightly in their proportions, stone may take on all manner of shapes and sizes, from precisely jointed, smooth-faced "ashlar" square blocks to irregular-sized lumps as are used in dry stone rubble walls, through to using uneven stone. Where concrete is used, we may be talking in terms of a molded, simulated stone block made from cement and stone dust, uneven like a natural stone wall. Alternatively, a basic concrete block wall may be rendered with mortar, giving a smooth, uniform surface. A concrete wall could also be made by pouring liquid concrete into a wooden mold or shuttering *in situ*. Texture may be given to such large expanses by using deeply grained wooden shuttering or by inserting wooden laths to break up the surface. Otherwise you could brush the surface of the concrete while it is still damp or "green," to expose the different colors of the aggregate.

A "cobb" wall (see page 34) is formed from mud, or more accurately clay, the wall being built on firm foundations of stone or brick. Layers of clay with straw and sometimes cow manure mixed in, are built up, then dressed back to a flat surface. When the correct height is reached the top is capped with a "roof" of pitched tiles or a pitched thatch. These walls will survive for generations, provided they are kept dry by their "roofs"; in frosty weather there is a danger that the surface can crumble if they freeze when damp. Such a natural-looking wall is most appropriate in a rural setting.

Mellow brick walls offer protection to this corner of a well-planted flower garden. The wall, built in Flemish bond and capped by roof tiles and a ridge tile, has wires to support clematis, Vitis vinitera *'Purpurea' and climbing roses, here 'Constance Spry' and 'Madame Grégoire Staechelin.'*

Building a wall

When an old wall to a garden starts to lean precariously, or actually falls down, or a new wall needs to be built, the first step is usually to call in a builder to take a look at it and to hear your requirements. You will then either be given a single quote for building or rebuilding the wall, which will contain all the expenses involved in erecting it, or you will be quoted a daily rate. The estimate will almost certainly seem colossal, but it is worth considering what is built into this figure.

To rebuild a collapsed stone or brick wall first involves clearing the site of fallen debris by hand, as many of the materials will be used again. Good stone and whole bricks are stacked to one side. Rubble, small material and old mortar are made into a separate heap, possibly for use in filling in the middle of the wall. For a new foundation, a trench must be dug and a coarse gravel base prepared and firmed before filling with concrete. Construction of the wall will then begin, building in regular courses, if mortared, and allowing time between every fourth or fifth level for drying and setting. Additional stone or bricks will be needed to compensate for those which were broken. Finally, a coping of some sort will be required to keep the rain out.

In terms of materials, cement, sand and lime, as well as the rental of a concrete mixer, the transport of

LEFT *An enclosed garden created from old cobb walls offers protection to rigorously trained fruit trees. It also provides a sheltered spot for a seat.*

RIGHT *Tightly mortared stone walling is a safe host for ivy, which furnishes this internal wall all year round. The wall material links with the stone in the path, used here with granite cobblestones. The wrought-iron gate opens on to a shady garden.*

Most wall bonds combine headers and stretchers in such a way that they are united in a strong structure that ties the two faces of a double-thickness wall together.

1. *Flemish bond*
2. *English Garden Wall bond*
3. *English bond*
4. *Stretcher bond (best for a single-thickness wall)*

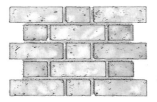

1

Building a brick wall

The strength of a brick wall lies in its construction—in the bond used to lay the bricks (see above) and the foundations upon which they are laid. Good foundations stabilize the wall, preventing it from sinking or sliding to one side. To give extra weight to the base of the foundations and to key them into the subsoil, a layer of crushed stone, similar in depth to that of the concrete footing, is compacted into the base of the trench. A concrete mix (of 7:1 ballast and cement) is poured on top of this to just below ground level.

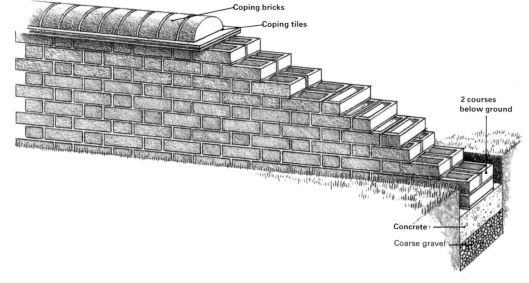

Coping bricks
Coping tiles
2 courses below ground
Concrete
Coarse gravel

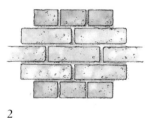
2

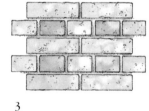
3

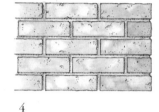
4

any materials and the clearing of any remaining rubble, will all be contained within the price besides the most expensive commodity—the labor. A builder giving a daily rate is offering his skilled time alone—everything else is extra and, of course, the longer he takes, the more money he earns.

Before accepting a quotation or employing a builder the question will inevitably go through your mind, "Could I build it myself?" The answer is almost certainly "Yes," if you have unlimited time and some practical know-how. An experienced builder, relying on previous knowledge gained while working with similar materials in a variety of conditions and sites can meet and overcome problems with relative ease. The amateur builder does not have this fund of knowledge, although he does have time to fathom out problems as they arise. If a section of existing wall is to be rebuilt, then at least a pattern is already established and may be followed carefully, mimicking the original materials in layering, line and style. If, however, you do not feel confident about undertaking the work, the builder's quotation may be reduced by preparing the site yourself at the outset and clearing the site at the end, bringing down labor costs significantly.

The construction of a wall

All walls should be built on top of good foundations for stability. A trench has to be dug first and the foundations formed within it. The depth and width of the trench depends on the height, width and length of the wall and also its function—whether it is freestanding, retaining a weight of soil to one side of it, or supporting overhead weight. The type of soil into which the foundations are sunk also has a strong bearing upon their proportions. With so many variables and the need for knowledge of local conditions, it is important to contact and take the advice of a reputable local builder before starting to build a wall yourself. To construct a high wall without the reassurance of a knowledgeable builder or architect could prove costly not just financially but, if it collapsed, in terms of life.

Stone walls Most stone walls use rough squared and shaped stone, which is laid in courses almost like a

WALL MATERIALS [Cost scale from 1 up to 8]				
Material/type	Cost	Aesthetic qualities	Ease of construction	Aging
Stone (mortared)	6	Strong structural lines, pleasing natural look	Semi-skilled; slow	Weathers well, taking on lichen
Stone (dry random)	7	Good textural qualities due to dark joint gaps	Skilled; very slow	Excellent, improving as it ages
Brick	5	Good—can be used in numerous patterns	Semi-skilled	Ages well but requires time to tone down
Reconstituted stone blocks	4	May have a man-made "regular" irregularity but often a good compromise	Semi-skilled; fast	Aging can be slow and less effective than real stone
Concrete block, rendered	2	Poor, but tolerable if painted a neutral color and planted	Unskilled	Poor, often not improving with age
Ready-mixed concrete	3	Poor, but acceptable if distressed or textured	Semi-skilled	Poor; looks drab on dull days and harsh on sunny days
Mud/clay	1	Good foil to plantings as color and texture are played down	Semi-skilled	Ages well, with subtle color change

brick wall (see page 34). The quality of the stone dictates how it is laid. If undressed, rounded or irregular stone is used, a more random effect is produced, with some stones breaking the regular coursing altogether. The wall will either be laid dry—without mortar—requiring greater skill and accuracy (see page 37), or with mortar, which can hide a multitude of sins. In both methods, the stone layers should be laid so that each stone overlaps the joint in the layer below. In most cases, a double-faced wall is built and the two faces linked with ties—a larger stone which extends the full width of the wall, creating a face on each side of the wall and binding the two together. The center is filled either with layers of rubble stone and concrete or, in a dry wall, with loose, fine stone worked in around the main walling stone. For strength and solidity, a dry stone wall is tapered slightly toward the top. This is achieved with the use of timber-framed battering boards (see right below).

Brick walls Although built from a regular, uniform material, brick walls may still vary considerably in the way the courses are arranged or bonded, and in their thickness. The different bonds are shown on pages 34–5. Bricks vary in their texture and color, depending on the degree of firing and the way they are formed. Although not usually cheaper, you may prefer to use second-hand, reclaimed bricks for their weathered, mellow appearance. Do not mix old and new bricks, as their sizes will vary. A brick laid lengthwise along the wall is known as a "stretcher"; bricks that cross through the wall with just their ends showing are "headers." Bricks often have only one good stretcher face, and care must be taken to use this side. Headers may be distributed throughout the wall to act as ties between the two faces and to give the wall increased strength.

Concrete block walls Here the components are considerably larger than brick or natural stone, allowing for fast construction. Building is a simple matter of half-lapping each block over the previous layer. It is usual to have only one block in thickness, but a very high wall may then require regular buttresses or supporting piers.

Faced retaining walls Where there is a change in level in part of the garden which cannot easily accommodate a grass or planted bank, a retaining wall is called for. A concrete block wall, formed by using wide, hollow blocks, is put in place first (see page 86). At regular intervals wire "ties" are half built into the block wall (as above). The wall may then be faced, to conceal the blockwork, using attractive stone or brick and building in the wire ties to connect the two together. For extra strength and weight the block cavities may be filled with poured concrete. A perforated plastic drainage pipe, run along the back of the wall at the height of the first layer of blocks and leading to a soakaway, will prevent water and frost damage. This should be covered with a layer of gravel, then topsoil.

Mortaring the joints

The finest dressed stone or the most beautiful small, pale bricks can be aesthetically destroyed by the clumsy application of mortar used to joint or "point" the brick or stone. Where excess mortar is daubed between the joints, the individual elements are lost, as is the play of light and shadow across the surface, and the whole becomes a single flat surface lacking life. When building a new wall, or repointing an old one, it is important not to bring the mortar flush with the surface and certainly not to plaster it across the surface of the walling material. If mortar is brought close to the surface, you should tidy it back with a small trowel as it dries, brushing off the remainder with a hand brush.

Finishing the top

It is important that a wall has a good "hat" and a good pair of "boots." This means it should have a good capping or coping as well as good foundations. A coping is a method of covering the top of the wall, to prevent water from entering the top of it, between the joints of the uppermost layer. An uncapped wall will deteriorate very quickly if damp has entered the mortar and is repeatedly frozen through severe winter weather. All copings should be slightly wider than the wall they are covering, to shed water clear of the wall's surface. The style of coping should be appropriate to the wall, and to its locality.

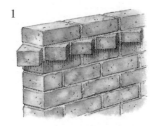

Copings protect the wall and shed water.
1. A line of bricks set at 45 degrees topped by another layer of bricks
2. Two clay pantiles capped by a ridge tile
3. Two courses of half-moon bricks atop a flat coping tile
4. A traditional coping for a dry stone wall

The simplest form of coping is a rounded hummock of concrete suitable for a cottage or house in a farmland setting. It is combined with the last two layers of the wall, broadening to form a jetty to shed water away from the wall's face. It is inexpensive and durable, weathers well, and can be used on brick walls or on dry or mortared stone walls.

A traditional, flat coping stone which overhangs the wall is probably the most widely used form of capping. The genuine article is not in fact flat but tapers to one side, shedding water away from the wall. Beneath the overhanging edge a groove prevents water running back underneath the stone, ensuring it drips off clear of the wall. The coping stones are mortared into place, with the joints filled and pointed. This simple, tidy form of coping will last indefinitely and require little maintenance; it suits a variety of situations and locations, giving a quiet, restrained finish.

A common coping uses long, thin, irregular sections of natural stone called "shukas." These are bedded on to the top of the wall dry or, using a sand and cement mix, positioned vertically close to one another like a row of dog's teeth, and overhanging the wall. Such a coping is best used in a rural setting atop dry or mortared walls.

An attractive coping often used in towns comprises three half-moon bricks, giving an architectural double rise to the capping. Undercourses of bricks

set out as jetties will throw rainwater clear of the wall. Used with either mortared brick or mortared stone walls, it makes an interesting nineteenth-century feature.

A broad, rural wall may be given a gabled appearance by using earthenware pantiles, one above the other, capped by a 'V'-shaped ridge tile.

This well-constructed dry stone wall has a coping of vertically placed stones which overhang the wall to shed rainwater. Bearded iris revel in heat reflected from the wall.

Building a dry stone wall

A dry stone wall relies for its sound construction upon skill and experience, and for its appearance on the quality of stone used. Traditionally, broad, flat stones laid on compacted ground create the firm foundations upon which overlapping layers are built. The center is at the same time filled with a loose mixture of small stones and fine rubble which supports the larger stones where necessary. "Key" stones tie the two faces of the wall together. A wooden frame (batter) projects the correct angle of taper for the wall.

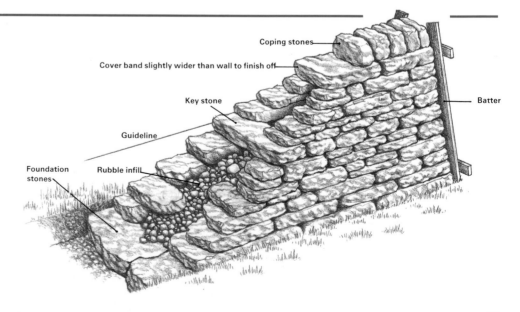

Coping stones

Cover band slightly wider than wall to finish off

Key stone

Batter

Guideline

Foundation stones

Rubble infill

Using walls

One of the greatest assets a garden may possess is a large expanse of wall, offering protection, warmth and shelter, a neutral backdrop and good climbing territory. The aspect of a wall is all-important. It is easy to list the qualities of a warm wall which faces the sun, but the other side of the same wall may have many negative values including low light levels, low temperatures and a damp atmosphere. It is crucial to use walls to exploit the conditions they create.

Plants used on or against a wall come into two different categories, climbers and wall shrubs. Climbers are those plants which have a scandent natural desire to climb: many of them will have specially adapted appendages such as twining stems (as in *Humulus lupulus*), aerial roots (*Hydrangea anomala petiolaris*), suction pads (*Parthenocissus tricuspidata*) and hooked or barbed thorns (roses and *Rubus ulmifolius*) to assist them. Wall shrubs are those which derive some beneficial enhancement from the shelter of a wall. In the main, climbers are, at least initially, rather more wall-hugging than wall shrubs, which tend to billow out from the wall. If you wish to disguise not only the appearance of a wall, but also its shape and line, wall shrubs are better. Avoid self-adhering, aerial-rooted climbers such as ivy on a dry stone wall and use only climbing plants with twining stems if they are frequently inspected.

The wall's aspect

The ideal wall faces the sun for most of the day, offering maximum warmth and protection throughout the year, and this is a site to savor. If it is an attractive, accessible part of the garden, you may consider an area of seating in front of the wall's protective influence, taking full advantage of the favorable microclimate. In high summer, the intense heat may justify the erection of a pergola, partially supported by the wall, clad in deciduous climbers such as vines (*Vitis* species), clematis and wisteria.

The aim here should be to provide the maximum growing space for plants. This may be the only area you have for growing so-called "exotics," so do not cover it all with gravel or paving to sit on. Broad borders beneath the wall, with a path or terrace in front, will enable sun lovers to clamber forward and over the hard surface. Be adventurous in this spot: try tender shrubs such as *Abutilon*, and wall climbers such as *Solanum* or *Rosa banksiae banksiae*, which in winter can be covered with netting, burlap, bracken fern or conifer boughs, if necessary. The majority of these sappy, fleshy plants are very fast-growing, maturing to flowering size within just a few years. They are therefore well worth trying—even if a severe winter should kill off some of the plants, replacements can quickly fill the space.

Another type of planting which would take full advantage of this situation is trained fruit such as

The wooden trellis fixed onto this brick boundary wall affords excellent support for climbers. The climbing roses which have grown above the top of the wall enable the adventurous clematis to scramble yet higher, giving additional screening from the adjoining garden. The semi-tender Itea ilicifolia thrives with the protection of the wall and surrounding shrubs, displaying its long, pale green tassels. The base of the wall is furnished in late summer with Anemone × hybrida, small-flowered Thalictrum dipterocarpum and phlox.

Wall supports for plants

All plants which are not self-clinging will require support to climb a wall. Galvanized vine-eye wall nails and strand wire are suited to climbing plants that produce few, but quite heavy, stems that need tying individually, such as roses and wisteria. Fix the wires 18 in. apart, supported by vine-eyes at intervals of 4 ft. Climbers that produce a fine mass of twining stems, such as clematis, honeysuckle and hop, require a freer run. They will clamber through wooden trellis or over coarse wire mesh.

Drill holes in the mortar for vine-eyes. Fix screw-end vine-eyes using a rawl plug in a hole drilled into brick or stone. Tensioning bolts keep the wires rigid.

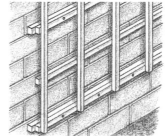

Screw square-section wooden trellis to battens already screwed to the walls to enable climbers to grow through it.

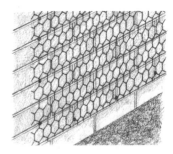

Wire mesh may be secured to the wall using long galvanized nails. This keeps the mesh away from the wall.

CLIMBERS AND
WALL SHRUBS
For a warm wall
Abutilon × suntense
  'Jermyns'
Ceanothus arboreus
  'Trewithen Blue'
Chimonanthus praecox
  (winter sweet)
Ficus carica (fig)
Itea ilicifolia
Magnolia grandiflora
Prunus armeniaca 'Moor
  Park' (apricot)
Trachelospermum
  jasminoides
Vitis vinifera (grapevine)
Wisteria floribunda 'Alba'

For a cold wall
Chaenomeles speciosa
  'Moerloosei' (quince)
Choisya ternata (Mexican
  orange blossom)
Cornus alba
  'Elegantissima'
  (dogwood)
Cotoneaster horizontalis
Garrya elliptica 'James
  Roof'
Hedera helix 'Sagittifolia'
  (ivy)
Hydrangea anomala
  petiolaris
Jasminum nudiflorum
  (winter jasmine)
Lonicera periclymenum
  'Graham Thomas'
  (honeysuckle)
Pyracantha rogersiana
  flava

peaches and apricots, which require early shelter and protection from the wall for their opening blossom in spring; a net may easily be draped down over the ripening fruit to protect them from sharp-eyed birds. The heat generated from the sun and held in the wall, like a night storage heater, will also protect any fruit over-wintering in a juvenile state, such as figs (*Ficus carica*) whose fruit take 18 months to develop and ripen. Some plants, like *Melianthus major* or the climber *Cobaea scandens*, need an extra-long growing season in which to flower, while others require their stems and branches to be baked by a previous summer to ensure good flowering.

On the other side of the wall, temperatures and light levels drop. This would prevent or reduce flowering in many genera, but there are a number of tolerant plants that will thrive here, requiring just these conditions, whereas they would be burnt to a crisp on the so-called favorable side. The emphasis should be on plants grown for their textured foliage display, as well as for their flowers. The foliage will remain fresh and bright throughout the summer and, due to the damper conditions, growth will continue into mid- to late summer. To lighten this area of shadow, choose some plants with green- and white-variegated leaves such as *Cornus alba* 'Elegantissima' or the evergreen *Euonymus fortunei* 'Emerald Gaiety'; golden-foliaged plants will also grow well here, reducing the risk of scorching on their delicate leaves, such as *Philadelphus coronarius* 'Aureus.' They will not produce the harsh golden tones seen in the open, but a paler lime, soft and muted.

Furnishing different walls

Shady house wall in early summer

A tightly mortared stone wall makes a good host for vigorous self-supporting wall climbers that fix themselves by means of aerial roots. Climbing hydrangea *(Hydrangea anomala petiolaris)* and ivy *(Hedera hibernica)* make a good climbing partnership suitable for a cool, shaded position, providing evergreen cover for winter and depth of color in summer. In winter the climbing hydrangea displays papery bark on its denuded branches, while in summer its pale to mid-green leaves provide a good foil for the lacy white flowers. Shade-loving plants furnish the house walls at ground level. There is a strong emphasis on foliage with the use of Solomon's seal *(Polygonatum × hybridum)*, finely divided ferns *(Polystichum setiferum)* and the variegated *Hosta* 'Francee,' intersown with the clear yellow flowered Welsh poppy *(Meconopsis cambrica)*.

Warm dry stone wall in midsummer

A dry stone wall with open joints, rugged in its appearance, must be planted with care to avoid the destructive personalities of some climbing plants. Those which produce aerial roots can damage the wall by driving their young growths into the unmortared gaps; as the plant grows and the trapped shoots expand in girth, stonework may be dislodged, leading to the wall's eventual destruction. The rambler *Rosa* 'Dorothy Perkins' makes a heavily laden climber, dripping with pendulous clusters of flowerheads. In early to midsummer the rose's strong pink flowers are joined by the bright pink pea flowers of *Lathyrus grandiflorus*. The *Lathyrus* uses the rose as a climbing frame, scaling it with the use of leaf tendrils. The passion flower (*Passiflora caerulea*) gives an exotic display of flowers, taking advantage of the favorable warm wall. At ground level the mound-forming *Hebe* 'Red Edge' complements the rose and pea in its leaf color. Next to this Jackman's rue (*Ruta graveolens* 'Jackman's Blue') brings out the glaucous tones in the hebe. Foxgloves (*Digitalis purpurea*) give early flower color while *Caryopteris* × *clandonensis* 'Kew Blue' will bring a late touch of blue to the border in early autumn.

Shady brick wall in winter

A heavily shaded wall may seem to present little prospect in the winter months, but with carefully selected plants hardy enough to withstand the winter cold an interesting composition can be made. *Garrya elliptica*, used as a wall shrub and pruned to retain a flattened profile, will be decorated with gray catkins at midwinter; its evergreen foliage is lightened by the leaves of the ivy (*Hedera helix* 'Glacier'). The oso berry (*Oemleria cerasiformis*), also trained as a wall shrub, will pre-empt spring with its young leaves and flowers produced soon after midwinter. A combination of hellebores (*Helleborus foetidus*), elephant's ears (*Bergenia* 'Silberlicht') and sweet box (*Sarcococca humilis*), with its insignificant yet overpoweringly scented flowers, create an underplanting of predominantly winter interest.

Choosing a fence

While a wall is generally a solid, closed structure, a fence may encompass many forms, designs, materials and styles. The structure may indeed be as solid as a wall or as airy as a cobweb, depending on what is called for aesthetically or practically. In a town or city, a fence is often there to bestow privacy or to formalize a vague boundary; it may have a purely ornamental purpose or provide high security. In the country, the same will be true but with an emphasis on functional fences to keep farm livestock in or out.

The many forms of fence all have their roles to play in different environments. What they have in common is slimness of form, which in a confined space can tip the balance between choosing a wall or a fence and, more particularly, between a spreading hedge or a fence. A fence combines the different advantages of a wall and a hedge: it can be built relatively inexpensively and upon completion it fulfills its role. There is, inevitably, a negative angle to using fences, which is that they have high maintenance requirements (see page 44) and a shorter life expectancy.

Suiting the purpose

It is what we want a fence to do that will to a large extent dictate the type we use. It is also important to erect a style of fence appropriate to its surroundings, or it will look incongruous. Careful observation of fencing styles used locally will offer some guidance.

A situation which demands almost wall-like privacy obviously calls for a closed or solid fence. In an urban setting, a woven or close-boarded fence may be used, to be screened later with plants to lessen its angular overall appearance. Woven fences, built from thin, interwoven strips of softwood, form a

FENCES AND FENCING MATERIALS		[Cost scale from 1 up to 8]		
Material/type	Cost	Durability	Aesthetic qualities	Ease of construction
Standard woven wood panels	2	Short-term	Rather flimsy, manufactured look	Unskilled
Vertically boarded	3	Medium-term	Good; may be colored	Semi-skilled
Picket	6	Medium-term	Good	Semi-skilled
Wood slat and wire paling	4	Medium-term	Simple but attractive	Unskilled
Iron railings	8	Long-lasting	Good in the right setting	Semi-skilled
Iron estate fencing	7	Long-lasting	Excellent, subtle	Semi-skilled
Post and rail (hardwood)	5	Long-lasting	Simple but attractive	Unskilled
Post and wire	1	Medium-term	Poor but unobtrusive	Unskilled
Chain link and concrete post	7	Long-lasting	Poor	Semi-skilled
Willow/hazel	6	Short-term	Excellent, subtle; improves with age	Unskilled
Fedge	7	Medium-term	Excellent	Skilled

Erecting wooden posts

Fence posts set straight into a hole in the ground and back-filled with concrete will be securely held, but will eventually rot. (Sink them about 15 percent of the total height, or 18 in., below ground, whichever is the least.) It is preferable to hold the post clear of the ground either by sinking a concrete spur in the ground, and bolting a wooden post to it aboveground, or by driving a pointed metal spike into the ground and inserting a square wooden post, screwed to the spike.

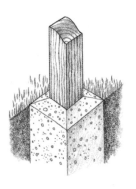

Wooden post concreted in position in the ground

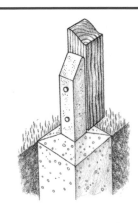

Wooden post held by a concrete spur

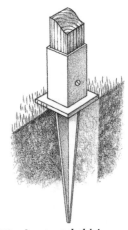

Wooden post held in a metal spike

complete barrier and a good backdrop for climbing plants. They come in panels of different sizes, which are attached to sturdy fence posts (see below). They may be painted with color wash (a thin, oil-based paint which allows the grain of the wood to show through) or stained with a wood preservative. Vertically boarded fencing gives an equivalent barrier effect and can be painted or stained if softwood.

In a rural environment wattle hurdles will form a near-solid structure; they may be purchased in panels of different sizes. Constructed from closely woven willow or hazel, they form a basket-like weave—willow gives a more refined finish, but hazel a greater texture. Their natural coloring forms a neutral backdrop to plantings. Wattle hurdles make an effective windbreak too, as they do not block, but filter the wind, reducing its speed and ferocity. Climbing plants keen to find a handhold are much obliged to the uneven surface offered by the wattle.

In towns and villages, where many front gardens no longer need to have physically strong boundary fences, they have been reduced to a nominal, decorative, demarcation gesture. Here the picket fence and iron railings reign supreme, their open structures permitting maximum light and openness while conveying a sense of segregation from the outside world. They both give an air of distinction to a property. Picket fencing consists of horizontals with equally spaced vertical bars giving a 50 percent degree of openness. The tops of the vertical bars may be shaped into points or fashioned into more intricate shapes. Stained, they have a natural, quiet look; painted, they become more pronounced.

Iron railings, whether elaborately wrought or plainly cast, give a subtle, sophisticated barrier, appropriate in an urban setting. They are expensive

A wattle fence, made from supple rods of hazel woven between split stakes, has a rustic texture and makes an ideal wind filter. The stems of climbing plants such as this rose (Rosa multiflora) may be individually tied to the wattle's coarse weave.

Fixing fence panels

Paneled and vertically boarded fences are vulnerable to wind, so they require sturdy posts. The post tops should be shaped or capped to deflect rain (1). Metal brackets must be attached to wooden posts before fixing woven or lap-boarded panels (1). In slotted concrete posts, the panels simply fit into a groove (2). Vertically boarded fences are constructed *in situ*, using square wooden posts with carefully positioned morticed holes to receive the rails upon which the boards are nailed (3). A metal bracket may be used (4).

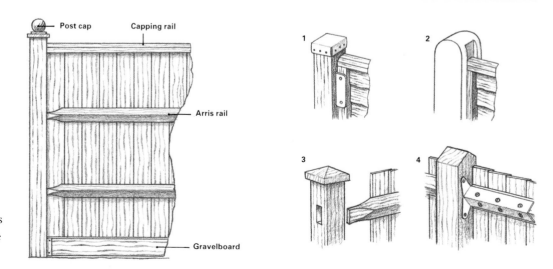

Post cap   Capping rail

Arris rail

Gravelboard

1

2

3

4

to install and must be regularly painted to keep them in a good state of repair and looking smart.

More suitable for the rural setting of a cottage-style garden, a similar fence to a picket is a chestnut paling fence. Wood slat and wire paling is bought as a roll and makes an inexpensive, easily erected fence, comprising two running galvanized cables into which are twisted wooden slats, which are often stained a red color. The open spars give a light, simple structure, over and through which plants may scramble, making a rustic effect.

Against open, agricultural land a fence must be strong enough to keep animals out, yet light enough not to impede the view. Here the choice is between post and wire, post and rail and iron estate fencing. Post and wire fencing consists of posts driven into the ground upon which unrelenting galvanized wire or square wire netting is stapled, giving a functional, light fencing. It looks discreet from a distance, the posts being the only clue to the existence of a fence. Of better finish and construction would be a fence of posts and rails, squarely sawn and erected, but from a distance this would be more obtrusive. Post and rail fencing, constructed from hardwood or treated soft-wood, is assembled on site, first driving in the square posts along which the rails are nailed.

Iron estate fencing is strong but light in construction, and if painted black it will virtually disappear; it makes an ideal boundary fence where you do not want to obscure a good view. It consists of flat iron uprights through which are passed thin, flat rails; the top rail is normally a round section. The four or five rails are graduated, being closer together at the bottom. It needs to be painted regularly.

If the tranquillity of a pleasant garden is threatened by the building of a new road, or the enlargement of an existing one, you will need to counter the intrusive noise and pollution. If space permits, a willow "fedge" would create the ideal barrier. A "fedge" metaphorically sits on the fence, unsure whether it is a fence or a hedge. Developed by a Dutchman but originating as a classic Japanese structure, it is a living fence made of willow: hurdles of living, green willow are woven and installed while still fresh and are supported by living willow poles driven into the ground. A double fence is required,

Trachelospermum jasminoides

Introduced from Shanghai by Robert Fortune in 1844, this glossy-leaved, twining-stemmed climber is much valued for its very fragrant clusters of small, pure white, fading to cream flowers. A most rewarding evergreen climbing plant for a protected position, it will relish the freedom to clamber through fine trellis against a wall or fence or up tree trunks.

with a 3 ft. gap between the two. With the hurdles held strongly in position, the gap in between is filled with good soil and supplied with an irrigation line. Leaves, then shoots, sprout from the hurdles, creating a hedge in a matter of weeks as it grows during spring and summer. In winter the "fedge" is trimmed back to become a fence once more.

Maintaining fences

Wooden fences rot and iron ones rust: these are the brutal facts about fences created from these materials, so some form of weatherproofing on a regular basis is necessary to extend the fence's life. The area of fastest deterioration is the point at ground level where near-constant damp prevails, but also where air circulation is good. This is where fungus attacks wood and iron oxidizes rapidly, so it is common to find posts rotted or rusted into two at this point, while above and below ground they are still sound.

When erecting a wooden fence, never economize on poor or substandard posts as the strength and wind resistance of the fence depends on these, much as a ship's sails rely on a strong mast. For wooden posts, use hardwood or preservative-impregnated

LEFT *Sturdy trellis used as a fencing material brings immediate privacy to a town garden. The wooden pier behind the standard wisteria breaks the line of the fence, making a decorative feature.*

RIGHT *A simple white-painted picket fence is appropriate for this country house with its wooden shutters.* Chaenomeles × superba *'Crimson and Gold' grows against the sheltered house wall.*

CLIMBERS AND WALL SHRUBS FOR FENCES
Evergreens for shade
Choisya ternata (Mexican orange blossom)
Euonymus fortunei radicans
Hedera colchica 'Sulphur Heart'
Lonicera japonica 'Halliana' (honeysuckle)
Viburnum 'Park Farm Hybrid'
V. 'Pragense'

Evergreens for a sunny fence
Bupleurum fruticosum
Ceanothus impressus
Hydrangea seemannii
Mahonia lomariifolia
Pittosporum tenuifolium
Viburnum henryi

Climbers for partial shade or partial sun
Akebia quinata
Clematis species and hybrids
Climbing and rambling roses
Passiflora caerulea (passion flower)
Solanum crispum 'Glasnevin'
Wisteria sinensis

softwood, giving either material an extra soaking in preservative the day before use. Pointed metal spurs (see page 42) will keep wooden posts clear of wet soil, rather like a shoe. This will not only prolong the life of a post but the eventual replacement of old posts is simplified by slotting a new post into the existing spur. Concrete posts will outlive any wooden or metal posts; aesthetically they are far less desirable, but they may be camouflaged by turning them into attractive pillars of evergreen ivy, clipped tightly to hold them in shape. Fine angle-iron stakes can be used with wattle hurdles, with wires holding the hurdles against the stake.

Painting a fence annually with preservative principally around the ground level mark will greatly prolong its life and should be done in autumn, when deciduous climbers have lost their leaves. Tar-based preservatives, such as creosote, should not be used near plants; even woody, bark-covered stems can be damaged by coming into contact with it. Oil- and spirit-based preservatives, though of shorter-term effectiveness, are less dangerous to plants. Iron railings should be painted with several coats before erecting them, especially around the point where they are inserted into the ground or stonework.

The base of any fence should be kept clear of the ground, even if only by the narrowest of gaps, as this will considerably reduce the risk of rotting or rusting. A replaceable gravel board may be used to fill the gap, to be renewed after a number of years, or a single strand of wire in the case of ironwork. The top of a boarded fence should also be protected with a capping rail (see page 43).

When painting or treating fences, bear in mind that the color or tone will dramatically alter the general appearance of the fence, if not the whole garden. Dark colors, which may seem almost black and far too dominating at first, will quickly lighten, merging the fence into the general garden scene. Lighter colors will only lighten further and, as they do, the fence will become more evident, standing out strongly against the muted shades of green and brown. Traditional paint colors for ironwork include black, white, dark green or dark blue; linking it with a color used in the house paintwork, or picking up the color of stone or brick may help your choice. To give wood an interesting change of color without obliterating its texture, you could use color-wash, which would give a distinctive edge to an off-the-peg fencing range.

Clothing different fences

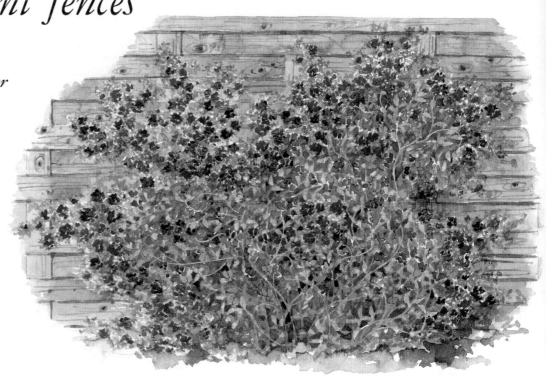

Woven panel fence in early summer

A ready-made woven-panel fence will bring
privacy and protection to a garden swiftly but
not particularly elegantly. The use of
evergreen and deciduous climbing plants and
shrubs will reduce the stark effect of this
angular fence. The evergreen *Ceanothus
impressus*, with its tiny leaves, will do much
to soften the appearance of the panel and the
small blue flowers will stud its spiky growth
in midsummer. *Lathyrus rotundifolius*
scrambles through the dark evergreen
branches of the *Ceanothus* in early summer,
opening bright pink flowers over many weeks.

Picket fence in midsummer

An open-structured picket fence forms the
ideal climbing frame for vigorous, fast-
growing plants which will clamber over and
between the pickets, creating an interesting
effect. Here the dusty miller vine *(Vitis
vinifera* 'Incana') winds between the decorative
heads of the fence, its silver-haired leaves
creating a light, attractive combination with
the darkened foliage of the honeysuckle
(Lonicera japonica 'Halliana'). This species of
honeysuckle sports one of the sweetest scented
of any honeysuckle flowers. *Eccremocarpus
scabra* produces muted red flowers over many
months, enhancing its summer growth of
long, trailing stems and attractive leaves.

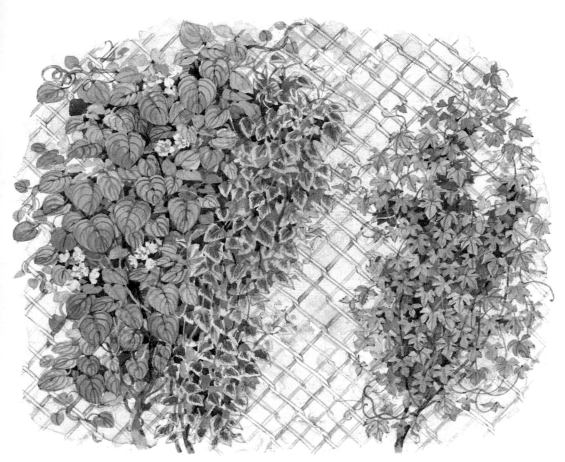

Chain-link fence in late summer

If you have a high chain-link fence on your boundary or perimeter for security, fast-growing plants will be called for to screen the interlinking wire as quickly as possible. Plants of a twining, weaving habit are best as they will run through the mesh, disguising a great deal. The herbaceous perennial golden hop, *Humulus lupulus* 'Aureus," will cover a large area after just one summer and in two years will hide much of the fence. *Actinidia deliciosa*, the Chinese gooseberry, will also rapidly weave its strong young shoots through the fence, producing its ornamental rounded leaves. For winter cover *Hedera canariensis* 'Gloire de Marengo,' although slow to start, will eventually provide an expanse of silver-variegated evergreen color.

Vertical board fence in midwinter

The strong lines of a vertically boarded fence can easily overpower a small garden, reducing the feeling of space. On a sunny aspect it is relatively easy to cover the fence with climbing plants, but even in the shady areas, which are often more prominent, cover can be provided by well-chosen climbers and wall shrubs. *Choisya ternata*, the Mexican orange blossom, is an attractive glossy-leaved evergreen shrub, scented in leaf and pure white in flower, which may be grown at the base of the fence or pruned and tied in flat against it. *Hedera helix* 'Buttercup' displays bright yellow leaves which add sunshine to the darkest of corners. Here it is combined with the winter-flowering jasmine (*Jasminum nudiflorum*), which produces sprays of star-shaped yellow flowers in the bleakest months.

Boundary and dividing hedges

A SHAPELY HEDGE

- The key to a well-manicured evergreen hedge is regular attention. This involves clipping once or twice in the growing season to build up a tight, close-knit surface lending itself to the creation of crisp, well-defined corners, tops and edges. (See chart, page 50, for the number of annual trims required.)

- Hedges clipped only once annually should not be tackled too early in the year, or regrowth will spoil their appearance.

- Hedges requiring more frequent trims should be dealt with when their growth is still soft, for comfort and for speed.

- You may need to use a guide line, at least initially, to create a level top for a long hedge. Make your own from canes and taut string; stick the canes in the ground every 6 ft. and check the height of the string by measuring up from the ground.

- On short, small sections of hedge, or items of topiary, you could trim against a hardboard template cut to shape.

- Once the hedge's line is established, you should be able to achieve a well-defined profile by eye.

To create a boundary or a garden division of subtle impact, and with sympathetic lines in harmony with existing planting, you may decide that a hedge is the best solution. A hedge can provide as much privacy and protection as a wall or fence, and has the added interest of seasonal variation in color and texture. Being a dominant structure, a hedge contributes much to the overall ambience of the outdoor scene, imposing a certain style on a new garden or emphasizing the character of an established one.

When used for wind protection in exposed areas, a hedge is more effective than a wall or solid fence; while these tend to deflect and divert strong wind, a hedge will filter and break up damaging fierce gusts. Planting a hedge is initially a cheaper alternative too, although in the long term it will require more annual maintenance than a wall or fence.

There are a few other disadvantages concerning hedges. A hedge is usually up to 3 ft. wide and therefore takes up more room than a wall or a fence, which may be a drawback in a garden of modest proportions. On a dry soil a hedge can create problems for nearby plants, by taking much of the moisture from a closely planted border. Yew *(Taxus baccata)* and box *(Buxus sempervirens)* are particularly heavy drinkers, which is one reason why the box-hedged White Garden at Sissinghurst Castle contains many dry-tolerant, silver-leaved plants. With deciduous hedges, there is also the annual leaf fall to contend with; even evergreens such as holly *(Ilex aquifolium)* and box discreetly shed their old leaves in summer, when the garden should be at its tidiest.

A newly planted hedge will, of course, take time to grow before it can fulfill its intended role and status, whereas a wall or fence creates instant impact. Interestingly, the hedge, such as holly, which is cursed for growing too slowly in its formative years, is the same hedge which, upon maturity, is praised for its tight nature and minimum clipping requirements. On the other hand a hedge such as privet *(Ligustrum ovalifolium)*, which takes off like a hare, is thereafter criticized for its loose, open growth and the need for constant trimming.

Choosing a hedge

The first decision to make is whether to use a single genus, to give a perfectly uniform hedge, or whether to mix two or more plant genera, to provide a lively, textured screen. Should the hedge be deciduous or evergreen? If there is more than one boundary hedge, should they form sharp, angular 90-degree corners with each other or should they meander, rounding off tight corners in the garden? These decisions can be resolved once the hedge's purpose is defined and the style of house and garden brought into consideration.

If the hedge's main purpose is to form a windbreak, you must plant a wind-tolerant species and, if you live by the coast, one that is resistant to salt spray (see chart, page 50). The hedge may have to act as a screen and provide privacy, rendering a deciduous hedge worthless in winter. If it has to keep out farm stock, it must be strong and preferably thorny, using for example hawthorn *(Crataegus monogyna)* or blackthorn *(Prunus spinosa)*, and it should also be free from poisonous plants.

You need to choose a species that will grow to the intended eventual height and width, and that will tolerate any adverse conditions of your site, such as deep shade or waterlogging. Once these practical aspects are taken into account, the final decision rests with more aesthetic considerations. A sharply cut evergreen hedge of yew will impose a wall-like, architectural formality, whereas a hedge of mixed genera, based on a predominance of thorn, gives an open, rounded hedge with a soft outline.

Single-genus hedges

Hedges composed of only one genus denote a strong boundary or division in the garden. Whether deciduous or evergreen, the effect is of uniform strength and solidity. Beech *(Fagus sylvatica)* and hornbeam *(Carpinus betulus)* are two deciduous trees which, when clipped as a hedge, retain their dead and drying leaves throughout winter and make excellent hedging subjects. Yew, holly and box, though slow to grow, make formal evergreen hedges, capable of

RIGHT *Enclosing hedges form a sympathetic backdrop to the well-stocked borders of this white-flowered garden, comprising Solomon's seals, astrantias, white peonies and hostas. Both beech and yew have a good texture and a rich color, and can be clipped to a uniform finish.*

BELOW *The rich tones of purple beech form a dramatic background to box-edged beds filled with summer-flowering plants including* Agapanthus.

being tightly clipped and even shaped into a castellated top or into ball finials. The evergreen species which make fast-growing hedges include privet, Leyland cypress (× *Cupresssocyparis leylandii*), *Lonicera nitida*, bay (*Laurus nobilis*) and cherry laurel (*Prunus laurocerasus*). They give a rounded, full hedge, though all require more attention in later life.

Flowering and fruiting hedges may be planted for added interest. *Viburnum tinus* and *Osmanthus delavayii* make early-flowering evergreen hedges, while *Rosa eglanteria*, the sweet brier, and *Rosa rugosa* produce a mass of flower throughout midsummer, followed by large, brightly colored fruit in autumn. The former has the added attraction of apple-scented leaves, most pungent on damp summer evenings.

As a low edging to a border or path, a hedge of dwarf box (*Buxus sempervirens* 'Suffruticosa'), lavender (*Lavandula angustifolia*), wall germander (*Teucrium* × *lucidrys*), cotton lavender (*Santolina chamaecyparissus*) or rosemary (*Rosmarinus officinalis*) make neat boundary plantings, growing no higher than 18 in. if required. Box is by far the most permanent of these, the others lasting from five to ten years.

HEDGE PLANTS						
PLANT ***=Evergreen**	**Leaf color and size**	**Flowers/fruit/ features**	**Annual growth rate/ expected maturity**		**Rows/plants per yard**	**Formality/number of annual trims**	**Tolerant of cold/wind (*=tolerant of sea spray)**
Alnus incana Alder (gray)	Mid-green 1¼ in.	Catkins in early spring; cones in winter	18 in.	5 years	Single (3)	Informal (1)	Yes*
* **Buxus sempervirens** Box	Dark green ¼ in.	Evocative scent	4 in.	6 years	Single (6)	Formal (2)	No*
Carpinus betulus Hornbeam	Mid-green 2½ in.		12–18 in.	6 years	Staggered (3)	Formal (1)	Yes
Crataegus monogyna Thorn mixture		Flowers, fruit and stem color	18–24 in.	4 years	Staggered (3)	Informal—trim once every third year	Yes*
× **Cupressocyparis leylandii** Leyland cypress	Mid-green ¼ in.		30–36 in.	4 years	Single (2)	Formal or Informal	No*
* **Escallonia** 'Donard Seedling'	Dark green ¾ in.	Flowers in late summer	12 in.	4 years	Single (3)	Informal (1)	No*
Fagus sylvatica Beech	Mid-green 3 in.		18 in.	6 years	Staggered (3)	Formal (1)	Yes
* **Ilex aquifolium** Holly	Dark green 2½ in.	Flowers in spring; berries in winter	8–12 in.	7 years	Single (2)	Semi-formal (1)	Yes*
* **Lavandula angustifolia** Lavender	Silver ¾ in.	Flowers in mid-summer; scent	4–6 in.	2 years	Single (3)	Formal (2)	No*
* **Ligustrum ovalifolium** Privet	Mid-green 1½ in.	White flowers in midsummer	12 in.	4 years	Staggered (3)	Informal (3)	Yes*
* **Lonicera nitida**	Light green ⅛ in.		12 in.	3 years	Single (4)	Formal or (3) Informal	No
* **Osmanthus delavayi**	Dark green 1 in.	Fragrant flowers in spring	8–12 in.	6 years	Single (2)	Formal or (1) Informal	No
* **Prunus laurocerasus** Laurel	Mid-green 4 in.		12 in.	4 years	Single (2)	Semi-formal (1)	No
Rosa eglanteria Sweet briar	Light green 1 in.	Flowers in mid-summer; fruit in autumn; scented leaves	18 in.	3 years	Single (3)	Informal (1)	No*
* **Taxus baccata** Yew	Dark green ¾ in.	Berries in winter	8–12 in.	8 years	Single (2)	Formal (1)	Yes*

Tropaeolum speciosum
The flame creeper
Tropaeolum speciosum *packs a powerful punch of color into the somber tones of a midsummer hedge. This self-clinging yet frail-looking climber from Chile will clamber up, opening delicate, pale green, six-lobed leaves as it ascends. Its brilliant scarlet flowers, once the plant is well established, will grow quickly each year from the herbaceous stock.*

Mixed hedges

Combining two or more types of plant in a hedge gives a more relaxed, textured appearance. It is not sufficient to simply use a color variation; for example, beech (*Fagus sylvatica*) planted with its purple-leaved variant (*F. sylvatica purpurea*) would give a dramatic color effect, but would lack character and texture due to the uniform leaf size and shape. But planting hornbeam (*Carpinus betulus*) with a variegated holly (*Ilex aquifolium* 'Silver Queen') gives a more satisfactory mixture (best used at a rate of ten hornbeam to one holly). In summer the hornbeam's green sward is interspersed with the lighter, prickly cream and green variegation, and in winter the golden-leaved hornbeam is lit by glistening evergreen panels. An excellent evergreen hedge which combines three slow-growing species in equal pro-

portions uses yew, holly and box. The color of the foliage varies from mid-green to a dark greenish-black and there is a subtle, varying texture of small to medium-sized leaves.

In a purely rural setting, a more natural approach may be adopted using indigenous species. If the hedge needs to be strong and impenetrable to keep out animals, a base of 50 percent thorn with four to six other native species randomly mixed in will give pleasing results. Field maple (*Acer campestre*), blackthorn (*Prunus spinosa*), hazel (*Corylus avellana*), guelder rose (*Viburnum opulus*), spindle berry (*Euonymus alatus*) and dog rose (*Rosa canina*) can all be used. A combination of these will give fruit and flowers as well as encouraging wildlife. Privet and holly may be incorporated to give a little evergreen interest for the winter period. Such a hedge should be trimmed on a three-year cycle, since regular annual trimming will result in little flower and fruit. Therefore, hard pruning is necessary every third year, to reestablish the line of the hedge; this will mean losing flowers and fruit for one year in three.

Planting a hedge

The ideal time to plant any type of hedge is late autumn or early winter, especially in the south, when temperatures are falling but are not too severe, with winter rains imminent. Spring is better for most northern areas. By planting at this time of year, the new season's bare-root stock will have just reached the nurseries, so there should be no danger of buying tired, dried-out specimens. When planted, you should be able to count on several months of rain and cold weather to settle the roots before they are expected to begin growth. The slow-growing species, such as box, yew and holly, are considerably more expensive than faster-growing hedging plants.

First establish the center line of the hedge using canes and string. From that, measure at least 12 in. either side of the line for the trench width and put down more strings. Dig the trench, as shown below, removing and destroying any deep-rooted perennial weeds as you dig. Spread a layer 4 in. thick of well-rotted manure or garden compost in the forked-over subsoil in the base of the trench to help retain

moisture and provide humus for young roots. Cover this with the fine topsoil that was removed when the trench was excavated, to a depth of 6 in. Into this topsoil carefully fork some organic fertilizer.

If you are using bare-rooted plants, leave them well wrapped in polyethylene bags to keep their roots moist until you plant. But if they cannot be

Hedges can be used to create inexpensive architectural features. Curvaceous beech hedges, clipped to form arches and corridors, need trimming once a year.

Digging the trench

For a single line of hedging, dig a trench 18 in. wide by 18 in. deep; for a double, staggered line, you need a trench 24 in. wide by 18 in. deep. Take off the first spade's depth, the humus-rich topsoil, and put it on one side. Make a separate pile of the subsoil, which is lighter in color and easily differentiated. Sprinkle some fertilizer over both spoil heaps. Partly fill the trench. Before planting a staggered hedge, as here, stretch two parallel guidelines 6 in. either side of the center line.

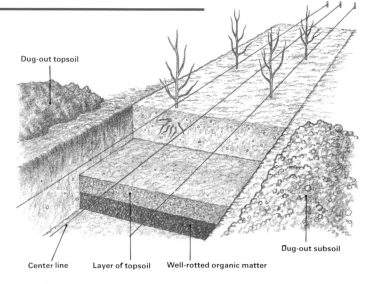

Dug-out topsoil

Center line   Layer of topsoil   Well-rotted organic matter

Dug-out subsoil

The distance between plants within rows can be measured off with a cane (see chart, page 50). If you have bare-rooted plants, you will need somebody to hold the plant upright, and correctly spaced, while you backfill around the roots with the remaining topsoil in the spoil heaps. Do not firm the plants at this stage.

planted on the day of purchase, heel them into a piece of open ground and water them. When ready to plant, lift and place them in a white plastic sack which will reflect any light and heat. Use the plants straight from the sack because the fine roots can be damaged by a drying wind in a matter of minutes. If some drying should occur, dunk the roots in a bucket of water. Bare-rooted hedge plants should be spaced and planted as shown on page 51.

If the hedging plants are in containers, water them well the day before. When you are ready to plant, remove all the containers and gently release any roots wound around and constricted by the pot; you may need to cut them with a sharp knife. The placing and backfilling for container-grown plants is made easier since the plants can stand where they are placed. The depth of planting is determined by the depth of the rootball: the rootballs should sit in the bottom of the partly filled trench, their tops flush with the eventual surface level of the soil.

When the full length of the hedge is planted, fill the trench to its brim with the slightly poorer-quality subsoil put to one side. Then check the level to which the plants have been buried. Often this will be too deep, in which case gently pull the plants up with a vertical tug, allowing the soil level to come just below the mark where they were growing in the nursery. Now walk the length of the rows, holding the tops of the plants, and gently firm them in with your feet. Use the remaining soil to fill the now-depressed trench.

After-care

If the newly planted young hedge consists mainly of long, whip-like sticks lacking any side growth, cut each back by at least half. This will ensure strong, dense growth from the base of the hedge. In its formative years a young hedge on an open boundary may be protected by a low-cost fence, which should be removed when the hedge is sufficiently dense. Where the threat is from rabbits or hares, which will eat young hedges overnight, you need to fix fine rabbit mesh along the length of the hedge, dug into the ground to a depth of 12 in.

After planting, the hedge should be mulched with mushroom compost, bark chippings, well-rotted manure or garden compost, or wetted straw (which beds down better) to a depth of 3 in. This will conserve moisture and prevent competition from annual weeds. Any perennial weeds must of course be eradicated as soon as they appear, particularly competitive species of coarse grass. If the weather is very dry in the hedge's first summer, it must be watered regularly, ideally by using a length of perforated hose, which will soak the ground without wasting a lot of water by sprinkling a larger area. The perforated hose may be left *in situ* along the length of the hedge, turning it on as and when required. A further application of fertilizer may be given in early summer, to replace lost nutrients and give the plants a boost.

Maintaining hedges

You will need to start trimming newly planted hedges before they have reached their intended height. Left unchecked, hedging plants will become sparsely branched at the bottom, with long, unbranched stems, unsuitable for a hedge later in life. From the first year onward, in early autumn, tip the branches, taking off about one quarter of the current year's growth, to promote side-shoots.

When the hedge is nearing its ultimate height, start to trim it regularly (see page 48). Hand shears will be suitable for maintaining a modest length of hedge and for trimming dwarf box hedges. With hedges on a larger scale, a powered hedge trimmer will reduce the length of time and the amount of energy involved. Electric machines are light and easy to use (always connect to a power supply through a circuit breaker for safety). Gasoline-driven trimmers are somewhat heavier but do not have the problem of a trailing cable. Always keep both hands on a powered machine. For the fine clipping of box shapes such as spirals and standard box balls, the scissor-like action of hand pruners gives even greater precision. Large-leaved hedge plants such as bay and laurel also need trimming with hand pruners to avoid unsightly half-torn leaves. Sheets of sacking or plastic placed on the ground will catch fallen clippings. Consider nesting birds and any fruiting and flowering subjects in your hedge when timing the cuts.

HEDGE PROBLEMS

- Depending on the species, a neglected or overgrown hedge will need severe pruning to restore its shape. Do this in early spring and follow it by heavy mulching with manure or spent mushroom compost, then fertilize with a blood, fish and bonemeal fertilizer. Water during any dry spells in summer.
- Yew, holly, beech, hornbeam, privet, laurel and *Lonicera nitida* can all be pruned drastically in height and width, to leave only main trunks and shortened branches, from which they will healthily regenerate.
- Box can also take severe pruning, although the results may be erratic. Some plants will regenerate well but others may die off and need to be individually replaced with home-grown plants.
- Conifers (such as *Thuja plicata*, *Chaemaecyparissus*, × *Cupressocyparis leylandii*) will not regenerate after severe cutting back, so you would have to replace with a new hedge.

Screening

(see page 55)

This ornate trellis screen placed behind an ancient apple tree partially hides a vegetable plot. It gives strong form to the garden in winter, casting long shadows across the hoar frost-covered lawn; the shadows are greatly enhanced by the "window" and arched doorway within the trelliswork.

However beautiful and natural an established garden may appear, close inspection will usually reveal several modern intrusions, present but carefully hidden away. Many of these elements are practical and of great time- and labor-saving benefit, but they are by no means ornamental and require some form of subtle disguise. Structures needing to be screened can range from large garages, oil tanks and even swimming pools to smaller hose reels and compost heaps. The trash cans across the drive, placed there for convenience sake, and large oil or gas tanks, again sited prominently for ease of access to tanker trucks, provide the most obvious examples of inelegant focal points. On a smaller scale gas and electricity meter boxes, often seen stuck on to the side of a building

like a limpet, as well as main water power standpipes and taps, may also prove to be necessary but unsightly additions to an otherwise attractive garden. Old adversaries, such as the compost heap and the tool shed, form essential working parts of the garden, especially in a large plot, but few could be said to contribute to its charm. Neighboring buildings may need screening, or at least to have the eye deflected from them in some way (see page 55).

Forms of disguise

Many unsightly features can be disguised with the minimum of camouflage; often it is necessary only to break the visual bulk of the offending structure or building to drastically reduce its bearing upon the

FAST-GROWING PLANTS
FOR SCREENING
Deciduous trees
and shrubs
Ailanthus altissima
   (tree of heaven)
Lavatera olbia (mallow)
Paulownia tomentosa
Populus alba (poplar)
Salix alba (willow)
Sambucus nigra (elder)

Climbers
Clematis montana
Cobaea scandens (annual)
Fallopia baldshuanica
   (Russian vine)
Hedera helix (ivy)
Jasminum nudiflorum
   (winter jasmine)
J. officinale
   (summer jasmine)
Parthenocissus
   tricuspidata
   (Virginia creeper)
Solanum crispum
   'Glasnevin'
Tropaeolum peregrinum
   (annual)
Vitis coignetiae and *V.*
   vinifera (grapevine)
Wisteria sinensis

Evergreen
screening plants
Elaeagnus × ebbingei
Mahonia species and
   cultivars
Prunus laurocerasus
   (laurel)
Sinarundinaria nitida
   (bamboo)
Thuja plicata
Viburnum 'Pragense'

garden scene. A solid screen, be it living or man-made, will tend to draw attention to a site rather than help to make it disappear, whereas a light, thinly veiled screen will make the ugly feature disappear into the background by confusing the eye.

Buildings within a garden may be well constructed and useful, but the materials from which they were built are sometimes out of keeping with their surroundings. However, much can be done to improve their superficial appearance, relatively inexpensively. Open trellis mounted on an offending garden shed or building will help to disguise the material from which it is made. It will also break up a large, solid expanse, giving a more sympathetic, textured feel by allowing for areas of light and shade. For a more convincing screen, which will also distort the shape and perspective of what lies beyond, use a freestanding structure. A screen for trash cans should

not be of a size that allows the cans just to fit in, but should be larger and certainly taller, preventing you from looking down onto the can lids. A meter box will be diminished by painting it a color which blends with the stone, brick or concrete on which it is mounted. If still objectionably visible, you could make a three-dimensional trelliswork obelisk and place it around and over the box, making sure the dials within are still visible. Generally, the darker trelliswork is painted or stained, the further it will recede into the background. In most cases a darker color works better at attempting to conceal, especially when used in conjunction with climbing and trailing plants.

The use of paint-decorated walls in the form of murals or *trompe l'oeil* has been evident in town gardens for many years, often to give a greater sense of space, but also to embellish a large, plain neighboring wall or to improve an unattractive house extension. This may take the simple form of painting on *faux* stone blocks or bricks, or may involve painting trellis and plants and windows. Personally, I believe this can be taken too far and that a better solution is to use *trompe l'oeil* techniques in partnership with panels of trellis, through which real plants may be grown.

Screening with plants

Where plants are to be used to hide an area or object, it is often assumed that they must be evergreen, otherwise the source of visual aggravation will be visible throughout the winter. But whereas a block

Trees and shrubs used together in a dense planting will form an excellent screen, if sufficiently deep. Trees alone will form high-level screening, perhaps suitable for extending a sense of privacy above an established boundary. The plant material used will be a matter of personal choice, coupled with consideration of speed of growth and, of course, suitability for the conditions of the site. Plants which will provide good screening within one or two years, like Russian vine *(Fallopia baldschuanica)* may, in later life, prove to be an embarrassment when they lift off roofing tiles, pull over trellis or rip up paving with their roots. Fast-growing species such as elder *(Sambucus nigra)* and larch *(Larix decidua)* will fulfill their

of evergreen shrubs, trees or climbing plants makes it very obvious that their role is to hide something, a mixture of plants creates a screen of equal effectiveness, but with less obvious intent. It is even possible to establish a screen built entirely of deciduous species, using densely branching shrubs in a suitably broad line—their fine branchwork will draw a veil over what is beyond, even through winter.

Used in conjunction with trelliswork, shrubs and climbing plants can add another layer of distraction to confuse the eye. Evergreen and deciduous climbers intertwined upon a trellis will give an ever-changing picture varying in its degree of cover, to be partially uncovered again the following autumn. A combination of plants chosen for variety, not necessarily of leaf and flower colors but more of leaf sizes and shapes, gives depth to your planting as large leaves appear to come forward while small leaves stay back.

role, some within a year, of providing good camouflage for unsightly features. These trees just need a little regular pruning to keep them within reasonably manageable proportions.

Where deciduous shrubs are to be used as a screen, consider a species with attractive stems or bark color. Massed plantings of dogwoods *(Cornus alba* cultivars) with stems of red, lime green or black look resplendent in winter sunshine if stooled or cut to within inches of the ground every other or every third year. Willows *(Salix)* will give a similar display of yellow and orange stems if treated in the same way. It is difficult to categorize plants which are "good for screening" beyond their rate of annual growth. Ideally you should use for screening plants that are similar to those elsewhere in the garden, in order for the screen to merge with the garden and not stand out as an obvious form of camouflage.

Gates for all situations

An open, wrought-iron gate is appropriate for both town and country houses. Here painted black, it does not fight for attention but provides a smart front entrance. Stone piers reflect the material from which the house is built as well as that of the path. Lavender (Lavandula 'Munstead') edges the stone path to the front door, while feverfew grows against the pier.

Gates take innumerable shapes and forms: they can be constructed from different materials, to varying degrees of rusticity or refinement. They may form the most elaborate tracery of fanciful decoration or be of plain boarded doors, but each has its place in the appropriate setting. In some cases a gate is to be inserted into a fence from which it will take its style, but there are many instances where gates are used in walls or hedges offering no inspiration as to the design or material.

The first choice to be made is whether to have an open, see-through gate or a solid, door-like gate or pair of gates. Wrought-iron gates are frequently used in both grand and modest situations, in town and country. The argument in their favor is that an open tracery gate allows the visitor a view through to the next part of the garden, linking one with another. I

rather like the idea of opening a solid gate or door to reveal a surprise on the other side. I strongly advise the use of solid gates at the head of a short drive close to a house where privacy from the road is called for. Where a fence or hedge forms a protective wind-break, if you use an open-structured gate for the entrance within it, you can inadvertently create a wind tunnel across the garden. Here a solid gate is a better alternative. If you have a slatted or semi-open gate, it may be closed in through the winter with boards, planks or netting, to be removed during the favorable months of the year.

In height, a gate should closely reflect the structure it is shouldered by, terminating at or just below that level. But if you want to give more importance to entrance gates, a pair of gate piers or posts raised higher than the boundary level will allow for taller gates to be used. A gate's width is determined largely by its purpose in the garden. Where access for machinery is needed, make sure it is wide enough to give adequate clearance. A frequently used narrow gate can be a nuisance when pushing a wheelbarrow or carrying a sheet full of bulky prunings.

Open-structured gates make a welcoming gesture to visitors when used as a front entrance, leading down a path to the door of the house. If a tall hedge has a solid door set into it, the entrance could easily be overlooked or misinterpreted, but an open, slatted gate, or a simple railed iron gate will provide an encouraging glimpse of the visitor's destination. Where a garden runs out into open countryside, or enjoys a pleasant view, it can be made to feel more spacious by leading the eye on beyond its boundaries. Here a finely worked iron gate will perform the role of a window onto the surrounding countryside. If used at the far end of a garden, surrounded by dark hedges or plantings, it will entice visitors onward.

Painting and posts
A semi-open boundary gate with distant views will retreat into the background in favor of a fine outlook if painted black or dark gray. If painted white, or any light color, the eye will stop when it hits this. A

front entrance gate may follow the same color scheme as the windows and front door to link it with the house; alternatively it may be painted white or another pale color to highlight the entrance. Wooden gates may be painted or treated with a wood preservative. I much prefer hardwood left untreated, to turn a silvery gray with age; it is drastically darkened after an application of preservative, and loses much of the subtle patina that comes with the years.

Gate posts of wood or iron, or gate piers of stone construction, contribute greatly to the appearance of the gates themselves. Square wooden posts are appropriate for a plain wooden slatted gate which can be attached by hinges and a latch. It may take two people to ensure that a gate is properly hung on its post. Plain posts can be made more elaborate by

cutting shaped finials into the tops of each one and perhaps painting them. Gates set in iron estate fencing and wrought-iron fencing should ideally have iron posts with ornate knob finials to complement the decoration of the fence and gate.

Large gates, or gates standing within a hedge, may be given greater importance by the support of stone piers, which will give a weighty emphasis to an entrance. They may be made of square-section walling stone alone, or of cut and molded, dressed stone, capped with high ornate finials. Look at other piers and gates before deciding upon the style, the size and, most importantly, the relationship and the proportions of gates and posts. It goes without saying that latches and fasteners for gates should be easily operated and, when secured, should remain firmly closed.

This white-painted slatted gate is entirely suited in both design and scale to its country surroundings. It forms a simple but welcoming entrance to this cottage garden planted with Linum perenne, Geranium grandiflorum, *pink* Centranthus ruber *and* Brachyglottis (*syn.* Senecio) grayi. *Wooden gates need good clearance, so they do not scrape on the ground when they expand.*

THE HORIZONTAL
DIMENSION

We may divide the horizontal dimension into two categories, hard and soft surfaces. A combination of hard paving surfaces of differing colors and textures with soft areas of planting, be it lawns or shrubs, will turn a bland, uninteresting garden scene into a lively composition. If the ground plan of the garden echoes the lines and divisions of the house in some way, this will help to unite the plot and to merge the house more successfully with the garden.

A paved garden need not look harsh, provided it is surrounded by lush planting. The rectangular pool brings an air of tranquility to this garden and the well-placed table and chairs adjacent to it take advantage of its reflecting surface, which creates shadows and a sense of movement.

Garden surfaces

The practical arguments for laying out horizontal features are a response to the physical demands on the site—the garden is required to provide a venue for outdoor activities. The hard surfaces, which will range from the narrowest of paths to large terraces and even wholly paved gardens, will be suitable for sitting and entertaining areas, hard standing for garden furniture as well as for cars, all-weather access for machinery, wheelbarrows and washing lines. Soft surfaces will provide safe play areas for children, in the form of lawns, as well as planted areas for flower borders, shrubs, trees, vegetables or fruit; they will also bring color and depth to the garden. Wildlife is encouraged into the soft areas of the garden even if it is only a bird probing for worms on a lawn.

Few gardens contain all the different elements that could make up the horizontal dimension, but in a fully developed garden, you might find paved terraces connected to grass lawns by straight or curved paths, passing by borders of herbaceous plants or mature shrubberies, while a side flight of steps may lead back to the entrance drive. All these elements contribute to the style of the garden, not only in terms of their proportions, but also through the materials used. For example, a large expanse of strongly colored red brick paving surrounded by modest-sized plantings will be harder on the eye than the same area paved in pale stone, encompassed by luxuriant plantings.

The lines that such features take will also influence the character of a garden. Straight-edged, square-cornered paths, drives, lawns and planting borders will endow a garden with a precise, formal backbone, and this may be followed through with regimented, accurately placed planting, to give a tightly formal character; or alternatively the formal backbone may be broken and softened by the use of informal plantings. At the other extreme, a garden composed of curves, circles and sweeps will give a greater scope for the imagination, but this can be overworked and may feel and look like the curved-edged pieces of a jigsaw puzzle. It is always preferable to use large, simple curves so that the eye takes in only one generous curve of path, planted border or lawn edge at a time.

Where possible, curves should have a reason for being there. The curved edge of a border may follow a contour, the base of an irregular bank, the foot of a curved retaining wall, or the periphery of a mature specimen tree's canopy. But if you have a totally flat site, some vertical features may have to be used to determine the structural lines of the garden. The width of doors, windows or walls of the house could be echoed in those of paths and borders; the width of the house façade itself could determine that of lawns, terraces or drives. By creating these visual links with other elements within the garden, a unity of form and shape is developed, linking the house to the site.

Why pave?

A hard surface may comprise six paving stones at the edge of a lawn on which a garden bench sits, or several hundred square yards of gravel, forming a forecourt at the front of the house. Both serve the same purpose—they provide a clean, free-draining, easily maintained, all-weather surface for parts of the garden subject to frequent use.

There are several other reasons for considering paving parts of, or even the whole garden. Areas of hard standing are essential for tables and chairs as well as for cars and garden vehicles. Occasionally, it may be decided that the only tidy option for a garden is paving, particularly in small gardens where deep shade is created by trees or overshadowing buildings, in which it would be impossible to establish grass lawns and maintain them in good condition. Any area heavily and constantly walked across, such as the entrance to a house, or the route from the back door to the lawn, or to more distant areas of the garden, is best treated as a hard-surfaced path. If the entrance comprises a small yard or courtyard then the whole may be paved, incorporating spaces for planting. When a paved area then leads on to a lawn, try to leave several routes through the planting, so that the edge of the lawn does not become worn through continual traffic in one place.

LEFT *The use of a variety of paving materials—here, multi-colored marble slabs with stones and stone paving—produces a surface rich in color and texture, giving this courtyard garden an exotic, Mediterranean feel.*

BELOW *Hard and soft surfaces are skillfully linked in this garden designed on formal lines. The precisely paved terrace and the immaculately tended expanse of lawn are balanced by the rigorously clipped dwarf box hedges. Within the borders, the plants grow in profusion.*

A specific need for paving occurs where a luxuriantly planted border meets a well-manicured lawn. The plants should not be chopped back to give a rigorous straight line while they are in flower, but if this is left until autumn they will have killed the lawn's edge by smothering. Using a path between lawn and border provides a surface for the plants to sprawl over, or you can lay a paving strip against the lawn to form a "mowing edge" (see page 85).

Integrating hard and soft elements

When planning the garden's layout and weighing up the options of hard and soft surfaces and the proportion of one to another, you should consider first their overall appearance and then the questions of cost and maintenance. The green areas, such as lawns, are the lungs of the garden. There is no doubt that the sensation of walking across a soft grass lawn does much to revive flagging spirits. Practicalities sometimes demand the replacement of lawned areas with

A cool and shady terrace is paved with roughly squared stone flags, forming a natural-looking setting for the eating area. This is made verdant by the abundant growth of honeysuckle, wisteria and vines clambering across walls, steps and their "host" trees. In a shady environment stone paving will rapidly acquire a patina of algae and lichen, with moss-filled crevices. Though attractive to look at, this makes the paving dangerously slippery when wet and will need to be cleaned off regularly (see page 104).

the detriment of other plants, grass edges and pathways, or will have to be uncompromisingly cut back from the border's edges.

Where gravel is used for a "hard" area, you can adopt a more flexible treatment of the surface. Areas to the sides, where traffic is minimal, may be planted with small plants which will thrive in a free-draining soil mixture (for suggestions, see the plant list on page 76); indeed, many will colonize these areas naturally by self-seeding in the gravel. A gravel path is thus made to appear softer and more friendly than, for instance, a brick-paved path with tightly fitting joints. Where stone and brick paving is used in conjunction with walls of the same materials, it is important to break these two hard surfaces with the softening effect of plants. Leaving a border will allow you to send plants up the wall and across the paving, to avoid a bleak, angular impression.

When comparing the price of paving or graveling an area against planting it with grass, ground-covering plants or a bed of mixed planting, you begin to realize how inexpensive plants are. It is possible to buy a huge number of plants for the same amount that it will cost to pave an area, allowing for materials and labor. However, you need to consider that a well-laid path or terrace should be trouble-free for many years, without further expenditure, repairs or replacement. The relative cost of different types of paving materials is indicated in the chart on page 66.

No planted area can be said to be maintenance-free, whether it is a grass lawn or a shrub border. Lawns need considerable upkeep, involving a regime of weekly care (see page 84). In some modest gardens, particularly in a town or city, a small lawn may not be considered feasible, with problems of shade from surrounding buildings and high boundary structures, as well as possible over-use. Where a lawn would have to be smaller than a double bed, serious thought should be given to other surfaces —for instance, gravel or brick. Shrub borders will also demand a relatively high degree of maintenance, with pruning, watering and feeding; plants will outgrow their positions, while others may die and need to be replaced. They are also subject to adverse weather conditions, needing protection against extreme heat or extreme cold.

paving, but even if the finest of old, natural, stone paving is used, the living spirit of the grass surface will be lost. If feasible, some panels of grass or ground-cover planting should be left to soften the paving and complement any areas of planted border.

Planting beds containing lush-leaved, herbaceous and shrubby material are the antidote to hard landscaping, which takes on the role of a foil against which the plants are shown off. A high garden wall, hedge or fence needs to be balanced by a border of a suitable scale and sufficient width. A narrow border can look mean and restricted but where, due to unavoidable limitations, small borders have to be used these may be made to appear bigger by letting sprawling plants grow across adjacent hard surfaces. The outer edges of a shrub bed can be widened as the plants increase in size, avoiding the sight of a ridiculously large, almost empty bed, until the plants contained there can justify it. If a shrub bed is too small and cannot be extended in this way, the plants will overshoot their allotted, confined space to

Paving materials

Brick, being a versatile paving material, can be laid in a circle around a central feature, as here. To avoid the tight rings in the center of the circle, a planting of saxifrages, thymes and Armeria maritima *has been made within a mulch of bark chippings. Surrounding borders are filled with sedums,* Dianthus, Rosa *'Zéphirine Drouhin,'* Verbascum *and* Chrysanthemum maximum.

Whether you are laying a path, a terrace or a drive, the choice of material, and the size of unit, will depend to a large extent on the scale of the area. As a general rule, the larger the expanse, the less fussy the laying pattern should be. Small paths can comprise a combination of materials and sizes, whereas larger paved expanses are better treated as a single surface.

Until relatively recently the choice between paving materials was clear-cut—if you could not afford natural stone or good-quality paving bricks, you accepted with regret the cheaper alternative of man-made concrete slabs at a high aesthetic cost to the garden. These slabs had a deadening effect on the area, not only from their drab color, but also from the monotonous shapes and patterns they created. However, such significant improvements have been made in artificial paving materials that they are now a viable alternative to natural products.

Some of the finest hard surfaces are created from a combination of two or more materials that are compatible physically and visually. Bricks or brick

pavers combine well either with artificial stone slabs or natural stone, to give a contrast in color and texture. Bricks can also be used as an interesting insert, or to create a series of panels in which a gravel filler is used. Stones, granite blocks and blue bricks used together will form a good combination of shapes without creating alarming color contrasts. Square-cut natural stone may be bordered by smooth beach pebbles, giving an exciting change of medium from flat, geometric rigidity to serried ranks of rounded humps. Always take care not to over-complicate an area as this would confuse the eye.

Natural materials

Stone Natural stone, although expensive to buy and to lay, is still a superior form of paving and, if locally acquired, it will harmonize with existing walls or paving. It takes on a weathered appearance more quickly than an artificial surface, which means that it always looks right in a garden. Old, reclaimed stone will already have a patina of age which will continue to develop. New stone will often appear stark for the first two years, but will then begin to mellow, building a thin veneer or crust of stone discoloration and lichen. When fully weathered, the surface of ancient natural flag- or paving stones is a thing of great beauty, with a texture of its own. Unfortunately, it is often the case that the more atttractive the paving becomes, the more slippery it is in wet or damp weather and in shady conditions an alternative material should be used.

Stone paving in regular units, often called natural stone, gives a well-ordered finish appropriate to both formal and informal settings. Irregular-shaped paving components, pieced together to form a jigsaw puzzle of different-sized pieces known as irregular paving, contributes a natural, informal look to the garden, giving an uneven surface free of regular lines and corners. But to create a level surface, great attention must be paid to jointing and grouting. This style of laying lends itself to a paving and planting combination, where pockets between the stones are filled with fine soil into which small plants can be introduced. Irregular, random paving requires a greater degree of upkeep as the smaller pieces of stone may be lifted by severe cold weather or shattered by wet and frost. When laying natural stone paving, particularly old or reclaimed stock, each piece requires individual leveling and different bedding depths of mortar to compensate for the irregular depth of the paving units.

Stones and granite blocks are pleasing materials in a paved surface as they have a rich texture, giving a lively quality to a flat area by catching sunlight and creating shadows. However, they are expensive materials to buy and also to lay properly. If they are inexpertly laid, they will look dreadful, with a preponderance of cement, but skillfully laid they will form fine geometric patterns closely butted against one another. Stones and granite blocks, especially rounded stones, do not make a smooth surface over which to walk, but they can be used for a paved area that has little traffic.

Bricks Paving with bricks is a versatile option which may meet many needs and create attractive paths and terraces. The small-scale components mean that little cutting is necessary, and regular-depth bricks simplify the laying of foundations and bedding. Bricks are small and light to handle, although they take twice as long to lay as the same area in paving slabs. Do not use porous or underfired house bricks for paving as they will shatter in the first winter of hard frosts. Use engineering bricks or highly fired bricks, which ring audibly when knocked together. Brick pavers, specially made for paving, are a different shape from house bricks, with a bigger surface face, but they are less deep, cover an area more quickly and require shallower foundations.

Bricks are available in buff, brown, cream, blue and many other shades. They may be laid on a foundation of coarse gravel covered by a course of sand and cement, or else be laid dry on a bed of sand. Bricks may be laid either flat or, to give a finer pattern, on edge. The patterns in which bricks are laid dramatically alters the look of the paved surface. Maintenance requires only the occasional dressing of sand between the joints and cleaning when required.

Loose surfaces Gravel is the most commonly used material in this group which includes bark and wood chippings as well as larger rounded pebbles and shingle. They all form a mobile and highly textured surface which allows free drainage for self-sown plants, and provide a simple solution for areas of difficult angles and slight conflicts of levels. A retainer or edging is required to prevent them from spreading onto borders or into other paving.

Gravel forms an inexpensive hard surface for drives and paths, but it is uncomfortable for areas where people linger, as on a terrace. It makes a crunching sound underfoot so it is useful for a circuitous path around a house, acting as a burglar deterrent. Fine gravel should be used on garden paths and a coarser grade on a drive or forecourt (see Paths, page 76). Bark and wood chippings are most suitable for a path cutting across a border or leading to a woodland setting. Rounded pebbles can be used as decorative corners to a wide area of gravel. Weed seedlings germinate readily in loose surfaces, and need to be raked or hoed out, or the ground given a herbicide application. Gravel is less easy to clean if full of leaves or if it is walked on frequently with muddy boots. An annual topping with fresh material in spring will renew these surfaces (see page 104).

Wood For occasional stepping stones through a border or wooded area I particularly like wooden roundels cut from a large bough or trunk with the bark still clinging to the outer edge. They form a discreet, understated path and allow plants to grow right around them. Hardwood roundels will last for many years, but remain slippery after heavy rain.

Wooden boarding, known as decking, can be used effectively as a total contrast to other surfacing materials. Evenly spaced boards provide a highly textured surface, ideal for linking a wood-clad house with a garden. Wooden decking has the unique advantage of being light, enabling its use at raised levels and across water as a "platform." Care must be taken when using decking in a damp climate as it remains slippery and dangerous when wet. Where soft woods are used, a wood preservative or sealer must be applied annually. Always seek the advice of an architect before using raised decking.

1

2

3

A herringbone or basketweave pattern (1 *and* 2) *will convey an old-world charm, reminiscent of the cottage garden, whereas a running bond* (3) *creates a sense of movement through the garden.*

ABOVE RIGHT *Contrasting natural materials make a practical solution in this corner of a garden. While wooden railroad ties form the main paving, rounded pebbles placed around the trunk of a mature tree allow it to increase in girth and help its roots to receive air and water.*

Man-made paving

Paving slabs are now available in subtle color ranges to suit the locality, and each slab has a color variation within it. They also come in many different dimensions which enables a random pattern to be established. With the use of rubber molds taken from natural slabs, an authentic, weathered appearance of uneven surface can now be achieved.

Small, regular-sized concrete blocks similar to stones or granite cobblestones are available in textured finishes, in different shades which can be chosen to complement existing stonework or brickwork. Belgian blocks, resembling thin bricks, create a fine-textured appearance with slightly chamfered edges. Pressed-concrete interlocking pavers achieve a homogeneous surface with only slight variation of color and form. This degree of regularity may be used to good effect in drives. On a small scale, the effect is of a modern, regular-patterned surface that is resistant to the softening effect of plants. A major advantage of man-made paving is its ease of laying due to its uniform depth: a foundation and bedding depth can be prepared to one level.

Tarmac or asphalt has an extremely smart appearance when well laid. It provides a smooth, regular surface which is neutral enough to remain firmly in the background. It drains well and requires little maintenance, apart from sweeping. It is a good all-weather surface suitable for a drive or forecourt, especially on a slope where gravel could not be used. However, it tends to give a municipal appearance to a private property—it is just too tidy and precise.

The juxtaposition of large- and small-scale components creates an exciting effect in this path leading to a doorway. River-washed pebbles and smooth pieces of slate are arranged in patterns around large stone slabs.

PAVING MATERIALS (Cost scale from 1 up to 8)				
Material	Cost	Ease of laying	Visual appearance	Non-slip/drying
Concrete paving	6	Fast and easy	Variable: some acceptable, others not	Non-slip; fast-drying
Granite blocks and cobblestones	8	Slow; requires skill	Excellent, creating texture and rhythm	Granite blocks non-slip; cobblestones slippery; slow-drying
Natural stone (squared)	8	Slow, heavy; requires skill	Excellent, clean lines; formal if required to be	Slippery; slow-drying
Natural stone (random)	7	Slow, heavy; requires skill	Good, of fine color and texture	Slippery; slow-drying
Brick paviors	5	Fast and easy	Good, creating shapes and patterns	Non-slip; fast-drying
Gravel/pebbles	2	Fast and easy	Good, creating a variety of looks with different grades	Non-slip; fast-drying
Bark/wood chips	1	Fast and easy	Pleasing, natural, soft	Non-slip; fast-drying
Wood roundels	4	Easy	Excellent in an informal setting	Slippery; remains damp
Tarmac	3	Requires specialist laying	Good, clean lines and levels	Non-slip; fast-drying

Preparation for paving

Any area of paving, whether a terrace or a path, must first be drained and leveled, then constructed to a high standard. Paving materials are long-lasting, so the length of the paving's effective life rests upon good preparation and construction.

The importance of drainage

Any problems with drainage and levels must be overcome before starting preparations for paving. There are several reasons why a site to be leveled and paved might appear wetter than surrounding land. If the garden adjoins a recently constructed house the soil may be suffering from severe compaction, caused by heavy machinery, preventing it from draining properly. This may not be immediately evident if the compacted subsoil has been lightly capped with good, open-structured topsoil. The problem may be rectified by loosening and lifting the soil, by hand digging on a small scale or, on a larger scale, by using tracked vehicles which spread their weight over a wide area without compounding the problem. If the loosened material can be left to weather down over a few months the soil texture will be improved.

If the land constitutes a heavy clay soil which remains saturated throughout winter and spring, the site might require the installation of land drains, or at least gravel-filled slits to remove water passing across a slope. Clay tile land drains have now been superseded by corrugated, perforated plastic rolls of pipework that are easier to install. They are laid parallel to each other across the site in a graduated trench surrounded by gravel and backfilled with soil. They feed into a larger main pipe which runs into a soakaway (a stone-filled pit or tank which then drains into the natural water course) or surface water drain.

Where a path runs all the way down a garden, an extended pattern helps to carry the eye along its length. A mosaic effect has been created here by setting different-colored pebbles firmly on to a solid base edged with a brick border. The linear impression is offset by the use of tall shaped hedges and rose arches (Rosa 'Alchymist' is seen here in flower).

Foundations for paved areas

It is essential to have a solid base on to which paving can be laid. Once the topsoil has been excavated, and the levels and gradients taken into account, this can be provided by a layer of graded coarse gravel. A grid of square pegs should be knocked into the subsoil to the finished level minus the thickness of the paving slab and the bedding material, to provide an accurate guide. Introduce a general fall by the use of a block placed beneath the spirit level at the lower end of the paving. Fill up to the pegs with coarse gravel.

Setting the level
Use a spirit level on a straight piece of timber to bridge and to check the levels between pegs placed some way apart: 6 ft. is a convenient distance. A wooden block, 1 in. high, placed under the spirit level at the lower end, is later removed.

The level of the paving needs to be established next. Over a large area, such as a large terrace or small paved garden measuring over 30 sq ft., it is advisable to use a surveyor's leveling instrument and ranging poles (which can both be rented) to establish a suitable fall of land; over an area smaller than this, pegs, a straight length of timber and a spirit level will suffice (see below). The topsoil should first be removed and stacked separately, well out of the way; all ground remodeling should be carried out in the subsoil layer.

Only a single, gentle gradient is generally required for drainage and it should obviously slope away from the house. As a general rule, allow a fall of 1 in. in 6 ft. for drainage. A much larger expanse of paving, such as a drive over 90 sq ft., may need extra provision for surface water: here, secondary levels are called for to direct the water away from the house, by coursing it into channels and then to a soakaway or surface water drain via a grilled drain opening. Such gullies and courses may form a reasonably attractive feature in the paving, particularly if you decide to use a material of a different shape, color or texture to form the gully.

These provisions may seem to be unduly pessimistic but they are put in place to cater for exceptional weather conditions. After a prolonged spell of rain, inadequate drainage could result in flooding of the garden and even the house.

A firm base

Unless you have a solid base for your paving, subsequent settlement will result in paving slabs and joints cracking, producing an uneven, dangerous surface full of depressions; these will collect water in wet weather which will then freeze in a severe winter, creating further damage. Any area that has been deeply excavated and backfilled prior to paving will be liable to settlement, especially where drainage pipes have been installed or where tree roots have been removed. On a smaller scale, it may simply be the position of a flower border within a lawn over which you are laying paving: the lawn itself should be relatively firm, but years of cultivation and inclusion of organic matter will have opened up the soil in the border, making it light and fluffy and therefore liable to settlement.

Wherever there is disturbed subsoil, action must be taken to reduce the risk of further settlement. Coarse gravel or roadstone will provide a good base if used to sufficient depth and mechanically compacted. An undisturbed site should have the topsoil removed, then a course of coarse gravel laid, capped with a layer of binding ballast or hoggin; this is rolled into the coarse gravel with either a mechanical vibrating roller or, for a modest area of paving within a smaller garden, with a more maneuverable, vibrating "plate" or simply a heavy wooden tamper, before laying the bedding for the paving (see below).

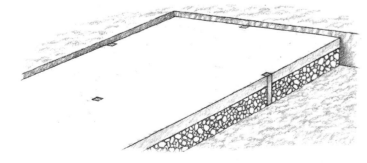

Laying the base
Once the levels are established, the area should be filled with coarse gravel and compacted with a vibrating roller or plate, then capped with a weak mixture of 7:1 sharp sand and cement. The finished level should be flush with the peg tops.

Bedding the slabs
To provide room for adjustment, bed the paving slabs on pads of sand and cement. When each slab is gently tamped down, it will find the right level slowly and easily.

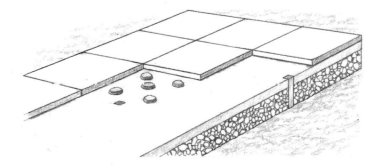

Laying paving

The method of laying paving depends not only upon the material in question, but also for what purpose the paving is to be used. An area subjected only to pedestrian traffic will be treated differently from an area occasionally used by a garden tractor and differently again from paving on which to park a car. A paved area that is solely for walking on may be laid on a bed of sand or a dry, weak mixture of sand and cement overlaying the coarse gravel and ballast base. Where heavy machinery is to be taken across paving, a dry, weak mixture of sand and cement is certainly called for. An area for car parking may have a concrete base laid on top of the coarse gravel, before the bedding course of sand and cement for the paving material. Strangely—and conversely—if bricks were to be used as the paving material for a drive, they could simply be bedded upon a sand base, to give a slightly flexible surface.

Small-surface paving components Bricks, pavers and cobblestones can be laid on dry sand to a level established by a secured row of edging bricks which will hold the shape and level of the otherwise loose paving pieces. Laying in this way is fast and clean, requiring only limited skill and the minimum amount of cutting. Butt the bricks closely together and, when the whole paved area is laid, brush dry sand to fill the gaps between them and to hold them in place. In time the joints will darken, showing off the individual elements within the overall pattern and creating a charming effect. (If you use a powered garden vacuum sweeper, care must be taken not to remove the sand when dried in summer.) Where services, such as manhole covers, are located in the center of a paved area, a panel of sand-bedded pavers can disguise and at the same time provide easy access for an annual check. Granite blocks, when used in a yard, drive or courtyard subjected to traffic, should be set on a wet mix of weak mortar and secured firmly before using a stronger, dry mortar mix to fill between them. As they remain securely in place, you can if you wish lay granite blocks in patterns of fans or regular squared bonding. Well laid, this will provide a surface of lasting quality.

Concrete paving slabs These are simple to lay. A layer of dry sand and cement is applied on top of a solid coarse gravel and ballast base. Before each stone is positioned, small piles of the sand and cement mixture are added approximately where the corners of the stone will sit, plus one pad in the middle. The stone may then be tamped down into position, the pads making for a finer adjustment. As these man-made slabs are all of a uniform thickness, repeating this action for each slab should result in an even, level surface. If possible, the joints should be staggered like a running wall bond (see page 34); they may be regularized by the use of wooden "spacer" laths to hold each stone apart from its neighbor. When in position, the same mixture of sand and cement is brushed into the joints; natural dampness from the ground and from overnight dew or rain will set the mortar hard.

Natural stone paving Natural stone slabs are more time-consuming to lay because they usually have only one flat surface, the underside being of variable thickness. The thicker stones should be taken as the governing factor, with the mortar level tailored to them; then each subsequent piece should be cut to fit and bedded at the appropriate height on lashings of mortar. When laying, try to keep breaking any continuous straight lines by using stones which straddle the previous joint in all directions. All stones should be square or rectangular with four complete corners. I particularly dislike the practice of notching a corner out of a stone to make it fit against another. The joints may be formalized with the use of spacer laths. With natural stone, I prefer sand alone brushed into the joints. Irregular stone has the same problem of uneven depth, coupled with irregular-shaped edges and it will take longer to lay. The pieces can be juggled around to fit together satisfactorily; they require tighter jointing than regular slabs, with less mortar showing, which gives a better appearance.

Stepping stones Stones across a lawn should be laid out in position and the lawn cut around their perimeter with a half-moon edging blade, then excavated to a depth twice that of the stone. After

Acaena 'Blue Haze'
A soft blue-gray well-ordered blanket of divided, toothed leaves is the main atttribute of Acaena *'Blue Haze.' Small rounded flower-heads and seed heads stud the surface of the plant throughout summer. Acaenas come from the southern hemisphere, originating in South America, Mexico and New Zealand. They are very effective when used to bridge the gap between border and gravel or to fill in a pattern edged with low box hedging.*

half-filling the hole with coarse sand, the stone can be tamped down into place. Like all hard surfaces against or within a lawn, the finished level should be just below that of the lawn to allow the mower to pass over the top unhindered. Stepping stones or wood roundels across a border could also be bedded on a pad of coarse sand, although it is also possible to simply place them on the soil surface, since it would not be disastrous if they sank a little. Ensure that the positioning of stepping stones caters for modest strides rather than giant strides.

Loose surfaces Any area to be covered with gravel, wood chip or bark chippings will still require a hard foundation if the surface is not to be trodden into the subsoil very quickly. Ballast rolled into a layer of coarse gravel will suffice, and a thin binding of sharp sand compacted into the ballast will then provide the ideal base into which gravel or other loose materials may be rolled. Edgings of timber, brick or tiles, or pre-cast, purpose-made edgings of concrete, are needed to retain the mobile surface. These must be secured by concreting all but the timber edging into position; timber edgings may be pegged down (see page 76). The edgings should be positioned directly on the coarse gravel and fixed in place before the ballast and sand are added. Any gravel edging set against a lawn should be below the lawn level yet still be capable of retaining the gravel.

Jointing The appearance of any area of hard surfacing is greatly improved if its individual elements are easily visible. This means that the joints should be recessed or raked, to reveal the edges of the material being laid. The result is a more broken surface with shadows cast into the joints. The best way to do this is to fill the joints to surface level, then, the following day, when they are still damp, to brush them or point them out with a trowel. Irregular paved surfaces may be recessed less deeply, in order to protect the uneven, more vulnerable edges of the stones. Materials that have sand alone brushed into their joints will need the occasional cleaning with a herbicide or with a knife to keep them weed-free, but they will be enhanced by a line of moss growing between them.

ABOVE *The rigid geometry of rectangular stone slabs is broken up by lines of smaller-scale bricks in this paved area. Both are simply bedded on sand, with sand brushed into their joints. A "mulch" of river-washed pebbles in the corner of a bed softens the harsh edge of the paving.*

LEFT *A radiating pattern of small squared granite blocks, intersected by blue brick pavers, provides a paved surface of a uniform color. The well-recessed joints emphasize the individual paving units, creating a well-textured surface.*

Enhancing paved areas

Shaded terrace in late winter

A terrace which has been a great joy in summer can be a bleak site in winter when herbaceous perennials recede and die away from the terrace edge and pots full of bedding plants are removed along with the tables and chairs, to leave an empty stage. But a lively arrangement of paving will give interest no matter what the season, and a careful choice of plants ensures a combination of shapes, colors, leaves and flowers all year round. The use of evergreens, both free-growing shrubs like *Daphne* and *Euonymus* and clipped shrubs such as box, will add shape and form to the winter scene. Containers full of evergreen plants with good strong foliage such as

Helleborus foetidus and *Valeriana phu* 'Aurea' will give weight and scale to the terrace, and could later provide color when planted with spring bedding and bulbs.

1 *Bergenia cordifolia*
2 *Brassica oleracea* (ornamental cabbages)
3 *Buxus sempervirens* 'Suffruticosa'
4 *Buxus sempervirens* 'Elegantissima'
5 *Daphne odora* 'Aureo-marginata'
6 *Euonymus fortunei* 'Emerald Gaiety'
7 *Garrya elliptica*
8 *Hebe buxifolia*
9 *Hedera helix*
10 *Helleborus foetidus*
11 *Narcissus* 'Tête-à-Tête'
12 *Valeriana phu* 'Aurea'
13 *Vinca minor* 'Variegata'

Sunny area of gravel in midsummer

A broad stretch of gravel edged with flower borders will present opportunities for allowing plants to spread over the edges of the border and across the gravel and letting others self-sow into the gravel. A well-drained site in a warm and sheltered spot will be able to sustain a silver-leaved planting, some of which may be of dubious hardiness elsewhere in the garden. Self-sown or planted biennials—Scotch thistles (Onopordum acanthium) and mullein (Verbascum olympicum) —give drama to the scene, whereas Salvia sclarea turkestanica billows out, with pastel shades of mauve and pink. The glaucous tones of Euphorbia characias wulfenii and Romneya coulteri merge to provide a foil against which the flowers of Linaria purpurea 'Canon Went' and Cistus 'Silver Pink' glow. The elongated flower bracts of Spanish lavender (Lavandula stoechas pedunculata) are shown off to good effect against the filigree foliage of Artemisia 'Powis Castle,' Acaena 'Blue Haze,' Eryngium giganteum, Thymus serpyllum and Erigeron karvinskianus, which all revel in the warmth and rapid drainage provided by the gravel.

1 Acaena 'Blue Haze'
2 Artemisia 'Powis Castle'
3 Cistus 'Silver Pink'
4 Erigeron karvinskianus
5 Eryngium giganteum
6 Euphorbia characias wulfenii
7 Hebe 'Red Edge'
8 Lavandula stoechas pedunculata
9 Linaria purpurea 'Canon Went'
10 Onopordum acanthium
11 Romneya coulteri
12 Salvia sclarea turkestanica
13 Thymus serpyllum
14 Verbascum olympicum

Terraces and paved areas

A well-sited terrace forms an extra room to the house for occasional eating out of doors or at least for a drink on a summer evening. For this a hard surface is essential, for a lawn will become damp toward the evening, even in midsummer. The ideal location for a terrace is a sunny corner of the garden, backed by the house and by a high wall, but you may need to site it farther away from the house to enjoy the sun and a more favorable microclimate.

The terrace which is to be used, rather than simply passed through, should be smoothly paved, using larger, natural flagstones, concrete paving slabs or well-laid pavers or bricks. Granite blocks, gravel or, worse still, stones are hard on the feet and tables and chairs will wobble on the uneven surface. A low or dwarf wall built around a terrace and topped with a flat coping stone will provide extra seating around the terrace and at the same time give the effect of enclosing the terrace. But people should still be tempted into the garden. If the terrace extends out above sloping ground a wall may well be unavoidable. If the change of level is minimal, a soil bank will be adequate, but otherwise a retaining wall will be needed to hold back the weight of the soil (see page 86). Here a broad flight of steps will help to relate house and terrace to the garden.

Integrating a terrace

When a terrace is located away from the house, extra effort is called for to ease the hard-surfaced area into the softer part of the garden. If it can be set against a boundary fence or wall, this lends solidity to the terrace and stops it from looking isolated. A path leading to the terrace from the main building will link the terrace with the house and its environs. A shade-giving pergola, clad with plants, will not only give a sense of permanency but will integrate the terrace into its setting of lawn or flower beds.

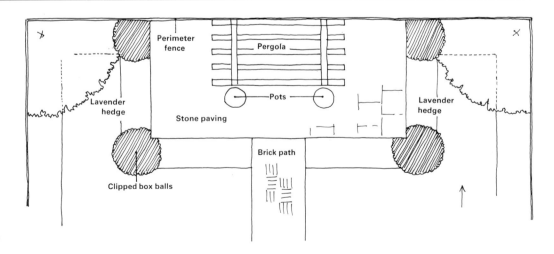

Perimeter fence

Pergola

Pots

Lavender hedge

Lavender hedge

Stone paving

Brick path

Clipped box balls

LEFT *This square terrace in the middle of the garden has been sited where it catches the sun. It needs the softening effect of plants around its perimeter to establish it as a firm, yet natural-looking, feature within the garden. Colored concrete paviors, the size of bricks, form a smooth surface to stand on and a pleasing and uncomplicated design. The variegated yucca offers large, shapely forms to the mainly small-scale planting of hypericums, helianthemums,* Alyssum saxatile *and heathers (Erica).*

Siting a terrace

Not every garden has an ideal warm and sunny area to the rear of the house, giving privacy and protection from wind; indeed some get little sun and warmth behind the house at any time of the day or year. In such a case, a terrace for sitting on must be built opposite the back of the house, to catch the sun rising above the roof. The positioning of such a terrace will be largely dictated by the size and levels of the garden but in general terms the farther from the house it is, the earlier and later in the year the terrace will remain in the sun.

Despite the inconvenience of its distance from the house, this terrace should still be made to form an integral part of the garden layout. If it cannot be set against a boundary wall, fence or hedge, the terrace area might be created half-way down the garden, perhaps linking it to a general plan of compartmentalized "rooms" tenuously developed from the house. If a more open-plan garden is to have a terrace sited at its center, the need for integration is even greater, and this can be achieved in several ways. A wooden structure of uprights and cross-beams forming a shade-providing pergola could be used to stabilize the terrace, which otherwise may appear to drift in an ocean of green lawns and planting. A hard-surfaced path leading from house door to the terrace will provide a dry, easy surface to negotiate when carrying food or drinks, perhaps in poor light. If complementary materials are used throughout, these will give another visual connection with the house (see left).

Bricks laid in an attractive basketweave pattern complement the brick walls and steps, as well as the terra-cotta ornaments and massed ranks of terra-cotta pots containing clipped box and palms. The circular, lily-filled pool, surrounded by a neat trim of ivy, breaks up what would otherwise become a sea of paving.

SCENTED PLANTS
FOR A SEATING AREA
Scented flowers
Chimonanthus praecox
  (winter sweet)
Clematis armandii
Cytisus battandieri
Daphne odora
Dianthus caryophyllus
Hesperis matronalis
Humea elegans
Lonicera periclymenum
  (woodbine)
Myrtus communis (myrtle)
Nicotiana affinis
Philadelphus coronarius
Rosa 'Ena Harkness'
Sarcococca confusa
  (sweet box)
Viburnum carlesii 'Diana'
Wisteria sinensis

Scented leaves
Artemisia camphorata
Caryopteris × clandonensis
Choisya ternata (Mexican
  orange blossom)
Eucalyptus camphora
Laurus nobilis (sweet bay)
Lavandula angustifolia
Myrrhis odorata
Nepeta camphorata
Populus balsamifera
Rosa eglanteria
Rosmarinus officinalis
  (rosemary)
Ruta graveolens (rue)
Salvia officinalis (sage)
Tanacetum vulgare
  (tansy)

A radiating pattern of pale bricks is broken up by lines of granite blocks, which are also used as a raised edging to this paved area. A well-planted group of decorative pots furnishes and breaks up the expanse of paving. They are filled in early summer with richly colored Primula auricula, *pale* Lewisia tweedyi *and dramatic lilies (*Lilium *'Côte d'Azur'). Box-edged borders give a tidy finish to the paving.*

The ideal size of terrace

It is difficult to recommend how big a terrace should be, as the most important requirement is that it should relate to its surroundings. Generally speaking, you should consider the largest area the site itself can take, without looking out of proportion to the garden and house, and the largest you can afford financially in terms of the cost of materials. It is fair to say that a terrace is rarely too big, as so much can be done to reduce its size visually. The expanse of hard surface will inevitably be broken up by furniture in the form of chairs and tables as well as by groups of containers, and any surrounding planting allowed to spill over the terrace will soften the edges and appear to reduce its mass.

It is a great asset to have a terrace spacious enough to accommodate permanent and temporary seating. A stone, iron or hardwood bench left outside throughout the year may be used immediately on a warm early-spring or autumn day, when the summer furniture is packed away. A sturdy, weather-resistant table may also be left out through the winter, and small containers of winter-flowering plants and bulbs may be displayed on it, to be enjoyed from the house windows. To establish an idea of the ideal terrace size, in relation to the number of people able to sit around a table, measure your dining room and see how that area would relate to your garden, by laying canes to delineate the proportions. If you have garden furniture, arrange this to allow easy access and room to maneuver, perhaps setting the table and chairs to one side of the terrace.

A terrace in full sun, backed by high walls, will in midsummer be a very hot, exposed site, sometimes too hot to sit on at midday. This would call for the provision of dappled shade, in the form of light canopied trees strategically planted close by, or a plant-clad pergola crossing the terrace itself.

Garden paths

An archway in a hedge of × Cupressocyparis leylandii *frames a narrow path, its rhythmic pattern of bricks and paving stones edged with stones. The path borders the lawn and allows the spreading plants to spill unobtrusively over it from the bed on the other side.*

Paths are essential to integrate different areas of a garden, but they can also play a more significant role in the garden's layout. They work best visually when there is a purpose to their siting or their existence. Paths which line up with doorways, windows or a garden gate will be pleasing to the eye and restful to the mind. A path without a guiding feature at its fore, or the influence of pairs of features at its sides, may be uninviting. Even a strongly variegated shrub or a tree with an attractively colored trunk can be enough of a focal point to draw the eye down a path.

Paths may simply follow a straight line between two areas of the garden, or may take a more winding course. A path which curves will look particularly effective when passing through an area of informal planting. A path of few but simple and generous curves, each merging with the next, is greatly preferable to one which kinks in and out like a snake. Where there is a natural undulation of land, a path should follow the garden's contours and create interest by climbing around it rather than cutting through its soft lines. One problem with indirect paths that meander around a large garden is that they may lead to short-cutting, resulting in worn grass or trampled borders. Planting rounded or prickly stemmed shrubs in strategic positions will help to prevent much of this damage.

Practical considerations

The width of a path is determined to some degree by the size of the garden and the "traffic" it is to carry. A large garden requiring mechanized transport would need a hard-surfaced pathway wide enough to allow a garden tractor and laden trailer to pass. Such paths should be well constructed for use in wet weather and at least 6 ft. wide. Main paths not required for access by ride-on vehicles should ideally be wide enough to allow two people to walk side by side comfortably, for which they must measure at least 4 ft. in width. Simple paths in a modest garden, as well as subsidiary paths which may cross wider paths, leading off into the sides of the garden, can be narrower—say, 28 in. wide. Always bear in mind that a path alongside a border will have to be wide enough to accommodate pedestrian access as well as tumbling plant growth. The width of a path leaving a terrace, opposite a door of the house, could be determined by the doorway itself, providing an appropriate link with the house.

To some extent, the width and length of a path will dictate the size of paving unit in its construction. A broad, long path is best formed from large, individual units or a combination of large and small elements, to give a repetitive pattern. Where large units are used, there should be not less than two components making up the path's width. A wide

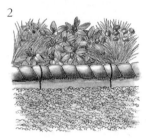

1. *Bricks laid at an angle, bedded to half their depth*
2. *Rope-twist clay tiles*
3. *Natural-looking half-sections of timber*

path built from small or fine-surfaced materials would look fussy and overworked, and would give no impression of strength, but a narrower path may use finer details within it to good effect.

Paths form the ideal foreground to a billowing herbaceous or annual border. Plants established at the border's edge can be allowed to fill out and fall onto the path's surface, softening the rigid line of the border. Their untrammeled, unrestrained sprawl will produce a memorable and worthwhile effect. Between a border and a lawn a narrow path can form a practical mowing edge (see page 85).

The best materials

Paths constructed from paving stones have a great permanency about them, unequaled by other surfaces. Those surfaced in brick provide an opportunity for decorative patterned ornamentation or simple, no-nonsense regularity, depending on how they are laid (see page 64). Bricks can provide a strong directional pull along a straight, narrow path, and may equally be used to accentuate the curve of a winding route. The small-scale individual components of bricks are appropriate for narrow paths of intricate design. Being naturally porous, they weather quickly, soon becoming a mellow-looking element in the garden.

A gravel path with a raised retaining edge of tiles or bricks on edge will create a good all-weather surface. But the type of gravel used will greatly alter the path's appearance, how much it moves and its durability. Pea gravel or pea shingle is almost round, very pale cream in color and roughly the size of a garden pea, which makes it attractive for garden paths. But due to its round shape it can be somewhat mobile and in dry weather tends to powder badly due to the relatively soft nature of the stone, the dust adhering to shoes and being walked into a house as white footmarks. A better gravel for paths and drives is crushed granite, which is a very hard stone; it is available in different graded sizes. It is a good color, a mixture of black, grey and white, giving a rich variety. The individual chippings are randomly shaped, which ensures minimum mobility and a well-keyed surface when rolled into a base of coarse sand. For a path it is vital to use only the bare minimum of any type of loose material. With fine gravels this means a depth of as little as 1–1½ in. Any deeper than this and one wades through gravel rather like walking across a beach, which is hard work, and the gravel is liable to be kicked and spread all over the garden.

Grass paths make a restful change from many of the hard surfaces already discussed and are best used to run between two flower borders. They will, of course, tolerate only limited use before they start to show signs of wear and tear and a temporary decline in quality. However, as a foil for well-ordered border

Laying a gravel path

The mobile nature of the gravel path means that it must be well drained and it has to be contained, to prevent the spread of fine material across lawns and borders. A base of coarse gravel is laid, to a depth of 6–8 in. (see page 66). It is essential to have a layer of 4–6 in. of raw ballast or hoggin beneath the gravel to prevent the coarse gravel from working up onto the gravel surface. Bed retaining tiles, stones or wooden boards into a concrete foundation wider than the path, before it dries.

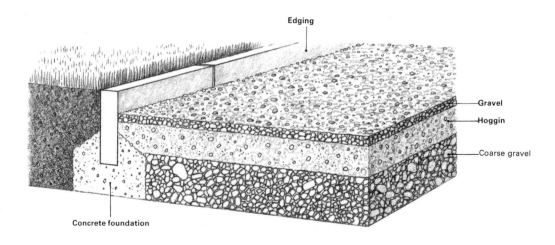

Edging

Gravel

Hoggin

Coarse gravel

Concrete foundation

RIGHT *An awkward corner of a garden is rounded off with the generous curve of a granite block path. The resulting deep border is filled with ornamental shrubs, some grown for their leaves, others for their flowers: roses,* Elaeagnus *'Gilt Edge,'* Cistus, Carpenteria californica, Brachyglottis (*syn.* Senecio) grayi *and* Viburnum.

BELOW *Sawn sections of timber known as roundels, mulched around with bark chips, make a harmonious path of stepping stones through shady planting.*

LOW-GROWING
PLANTS FOR PAVING
Acaena 'Blue Haze'
Chamomile nobile
  'Treneague'
Raoulia australis
Sagina subulata
Sedum acre
Soleirolia soleirolii
Thymus serpyllum

SELF-SEEDING
PLANTS FOR GRAVEL
Centranthus ruber
Erigeron karvinskianus
Eryngium giganteum
Oenothera biennis
Onopordum acanthium
Salvia sclarea
  turkestanica
Sisyrinchium striatum
Verbascum olympicum

plants, a grass path is unbeatable, if relatively impractical as the plants will always wish to grow over the edges. It is helpful if you can to make life easier for yourself and the mower by avoiding awkward shapes and corners and by tailoring the width of a grass path to multiples of the mower's width: complete stripes will look a lot tidier than the odd half-stripe.

The initial outlay is minimal, although of course maintenance is high: apart from weekly mowing in summer, the edges must be kept sheared neatly back at regular intervals unless they have edging stones over which the mower can run. A hard-wearing grass seed mixture will give added durability to a vulnerable surface. You need to decide whether rye grass (a most vigorous grass species) is to be included for its extra hard-wearing quality (it is baseball- and football-tolerant) against the drawback of its fast growth, needing frequent mowing. A mixture containing 40 percent rye grass, 55 percent fescue, and 5 percent bent will give hard-wearing qualities without the excessive growth of rye grass.

Paths bordered by plants

Shady brick path in early summer

This path gently curves its way beneath trees underplanted with shade-loving species. Plants tumble exuberantly over the path's edge, behind which well-foliaged, flowering herbaceous plants combine to give a patchwork of shapes and colors. The rich, fresh green of hardy ferns is echoed in the flower color of the euphorbias. Low edging plants skirting the path, including lily of the valley, the neat little *Hosta* 'Mrs. Field Fisher' and *Geranium renardii*, provide a ruff of low cover. *Cimicifuga racemosa* creates height in the borders while *Smilacina racemosa* and *Polygonatum × hybrida* give bulk to the planting.

1 *Cimicifuga racemosa*
2 *Convallaria majalis*
3 *Euphorbia amygdaloides robbiae*
4 *Euphorbia palustris*
5 *Geranium renardii*
6 *Hosta* 'Mrs. Field Fisher'
7 *Matteuccia struthiopteris*
8 *Polygonatum × hybrida*
9 *Polystichum setiferum*
10 *Pulmonaria angustifolia*
11 *Smilacina racemosa*
12 *Tiarella cordifolia*

Stone-flagged sunny path in early summer

A color-themed planting edges this weathered stone path. The muted tones of purple and mauve merge harmoniously while each plant provides a contrast of form and a foil for its neighbor. The leaden coloring of *Erysimum* 'Bowles' Mauve' and *Salvia officinalis* 'Purpurascens' create the ideal foreground planting for the flowers of the *Campanula*, *Allium* and the *Papaver orientale* 'Mrs. Marrow's Plum' seen above them. Groupings of *Atriplex hortensis*, *Weigela florida*, *Fuchsia magellanica* and *Hebe* 'Mrs. Winder' will all intensify the theme of purple, as will the deep-purple flowered *Penstemon* 'Raven' and *Sedum* 'Ruby Glow.'

Sunny path of granite blocks in early summer

With the use of quiet, yet well-textured plants the appearance of the square, gray blocks is reduced in severity. *Santolina chamaecyparissus* and *Ruta graveolens* form mounds of attractive silver foliage. *Sedum spectabile* 'Autumn Joy' produces succulent pale green leaves on stocky plants which look tidy all summer long, finally flowering at its end. Pale blue *Viola cornuta* trails and threads its way between edging plants of lavender and the globular-flower-headed *Nepeta nervosa*. The tall ornamental onion, *Allium aflatunense*, emerges to lend color and form to the neighboring planting, *Artemisia arborescens* and *Perovskia* providing an effective backdrop. Both *Melianthus major* and *Acanthus spinosus* contribute fine architectural leaves.

1 *Acanthus spinosus*
2 *Allium aflatunense*
3 *Artemisia arborescens*
4 *Lavandula angustifolia* 'Munstead'
5 *Melianthus major*
6 *Nepeta nervosa*
7 *Perovskia* 'Blue Spire'
8 *Rosa* 'Ballerina'
9 *Ruta graveolens* 'Jackman's Blue'
10 *Santolina chamaecyparissus*
11 *Sedum spectabile* 'Autumn Joy'
12 *Stachys byzantina* 'Sheila McQueen'
13 *Viola cornuta*

1 *Allium aflatunense* 'Purple Sensation'
2 *Atriplex hortensis*
3 *Campanula latiloba* 'Hidcote Amethyst'
4 *Cistus purpureus*
5 *Erysimum* 'Bowles' Mauve'
6 *Fuchsia magellanica* 'Versicolor'
7 *Hebe* 'Mrs. Winder'
8 *Lavandula stoechas*
9 *Papaver orientale* 'Mrs. Marrow's Plum'
10 *Penstemon* 'Raven'
11 *Salvia officinalis* 'Purpurascens'
12 *Sedum maximum* 'Atropurpureum'
13 *Viola labradorica*
14 *Weigela florida* 'Foliis Purpureis'

Drives and entrances

The rigid lines of a graveled approach to a house are softened by thoughtful planting which masks the drive's functional role. A line of small trees and large shrubs fringe the drive, obscuring the garden beyond yet offering a glimpse of the intended destination—the house. The edge of the drive is lost in a foaming mass of Alchemilla mollis, which spills onto the gravel, backed by the taller, bright yellow spires of Lysimachia punctata.

The entrance and drive to a property conveys an immediate impression of a garden and house, be it one of care and attention to detail or one of disinterest and neglect. It is, therefore, important that this area is given the same consideration as the rest of the garden and is not overlooked, even though it may be a more open public place. Try to look at the entrance with new eyes, as the first-time visitor would, and appraise it accordingly.

The focus of attention in a drive is usually the car, and this will dictate several requirements. The drive and its entrance must be wide enough for easy access, and the surface must in all weathers be fit to take the weight and maneuvering abrasion of rubber tires. Ideally, enough room for turning the car should be provided, in the form of a large enough turning circle, a turning and reversing bay, or a drive extension to allow a car to pass out of a second gate. However, do not let the car design your entire approach to the front of the house—it should be catered to, but not pandered to.

It is difficult to define the amount of space to allocate to a drive and perhaps forecourt in the abstract, with every house and garden varying in size and shape and angle. But its dimensions should reflect the size and number of cars most frequently used. As a guide, the average car measures 13 ft. in length and 5 ft. in width and will require a turning circle of not less than 39 ft. in diameter. A large turning forecourt at the front of a house may be of great use but it can all too easily start to look like a public parking lot of open, barren terrain. The visual impact of the broad expanse of hard surface should be reduced where possible and here the paving material used is of great significance. An unbroken expanse, uniform in its coloring and texture, will appear considerably larger and quite unrelenting in its form when compared with a more irregular surface, where sunlight and shadows interrupt the monotony. Tarmac or poured concrete will give a long-lasting, easily maintained surface, but one of limited visual charm, whereas a surface laid with gravel, granite blocks, or brick pavers would help to reduce the visual scale of the area, making a lively composition and a more domestic setting.

Integrating plants

The shape of a drive may be masked by the use of plants. If you find an existing open drive or forecourt too large it can be reduced by planting spreading shrubs at the sides, to cut down the overall area of hard surface, or by creating an "island" in the center of the hard surface. But how do we know how much drive we can spare, and if an island oasis will still permit easy maneuverability on a dark wet night? The answer is to experiment with mobile obstructions placed along the lines and curves of your proposed amendments. Use firewood logs, soil-filled plastic pots or bricks stood on end and, ideally, leave the obstructions in place for several weeks to evaluate the reduced space. Adjust any line where the objects are hit with regularity until it is more satisfactory.

An island should preferably be round or oval in shape and be finished with a solid edging of granite

POLLUTION-TOLERANT
PLANTS FOR DRIVES
Aesculus hippocastanum
Amelanchier species
Aralia elata
Aucuba japonica
Buxus sempervirens
Chaenomeles speciosa
Cornus alba
Elaeagnus × ebbingei
Euonymus fortunei
Fatsia japonica
Hydrangea macrophylla
Ilex aquifolium
Lonicera pileata
Mahonia × media
Malus hupehensis
Morus nigra
Rhus glabra
Skimmia japonica
Tilia × euchlora

blocks, brick or concrete curb to retain it and prevent damage by vehicles. It may be simply grassed, planted with an assortment of shrubs and ground-covering plants, or grassed and centrally planted with a single specimen tree. When using anything other than grass you need to ensure that the excava-tions extend beyond the drive footings into natural subsoil, otherwise the plantings will be sitting in a large container vulnerable to drying out or waterlog-ging. The soil level may be left flat or raised in a gentle mound; if possible, allow time for settlement before planting, seeding or sodding.

The sides of the drive may be grassed or planted, or both. An edge of well-mown sod will further emphasise the drive's outline, whereas a shrub planting can do much to lose its hard lines, with softening foliage and growth. As the plants around the drive and leading to the front door are seen every day, some all-year-round interest should be sought. A balance of deciduous and evergreen shrubs will give seasonal variety; flowering shrubs carrying berries through into the first months of winter will be attractive at the bleakest time of the year; and trees and shrubs with colorful stems or trunks should be included for months of dramatic impact.

To mark a darkened drive, choose plants with pale or white flowers, berries, stems or trunks for around the edges. When a car's headlights strike the gleam-ing white trunks of *Betula utilis jacquemontii*, or the ghostly-pale stems of *Rubus cockburnianus*, this helps the traveler to orientate himself or herself. A group planting of *Rosa* 'Nevada' by a front door would highlight the entrance, albeit fleetingly, with its large spreads of cream, single flowers. You may wish to select only pollution-tolerant species to withstand the gasoline fumes, and several are given in the plant list on this page. A little importance should always be given to the approach and the front door itself, emphasizing this as the main entrance to the house. This is often practiced by placing a pair of con-tainers, small trees, shrubs or topiary on either side of the approach path or the doorway itself.

Well-planted containers and a combination of contrasting paving materials create a sophisticated entrance to a modern house. The brick-paved approach is comfortable to walk on and does not risk becoming slippery when wet as it is protected by a canopy extending from the house. The cobblestones and marble slabs create a well-textured surface for an area taking less traffic.

Lawns and grassed areas

terraces, will by comparison have a frenetic, "busy" feeling, an unrestful personality. The introduction of even a small area of lawn into this garden will provide an area of calm and contrast.

How much lawn?

Where possible, the size of a lawn should reflect the size of the house or at least its façade. A large house may have small lawns close to the house broken up by paths, terraces and borders of plantings, but farther away an expansive lawn is important to provide views from the house, and back to the house from the garden. A smaller plot may have room for only one area of grass, and here the keen gardener and plantsperson will be greatly exercised by the range of plants available to the limited planting areas which threaten to engulf the lawn, if borders are widened. A balance must be established between lawns and planting in your basic plan and strictly adhered to. For children, a lawn is virtually a necessity, providing a soft and safe play surface for the summer months, capable of regeneration and self-repair after the hardest of use.

In comparison with establishing a large planted or hard-surfaced area, an expanse of lawn is a relatively inexpensive option to take. I would certainly recommend the owner of a newly built house with a blank space for a garden to contemplate grassing the entire plot, providing time to ponder the garden's possibilities over one year. By doing so, you create a single plane, enabling you to think clearly about the opportunities offered by the site. Where planted borders are subsequently made, the sod may be incorporated, greatly enhancing the soil structure.

Several more mundane facts make areas of grass a sensible choice. A garden liable to flooding, or at least with above-average rainfall, would do well to retain areas of grass for rapid absorption and drainage. Wherever trees and large shrubs are growing, lawns beneath and around them make for a safe, undisturbed environment away from the gardener's fork and hoe, and from herbicides that may be sprayed on gravel, paving or flower borders.

It is all too easy to take an area of lawn for granted, but lawns are unequaled in establishing a fine foreground of subtle and tranquil character which allows other features, such as plants, to take center stage. The flowering ornamental crab apples (Malus floribunda), *copper beech, Judas tree* (Cercis siliquastrum) *and pendulous flowered* Magnolia wilsonii *make a fine combination.*

The lawn could be said to be a scene-setter. No matter how fine the paved surfaces, or how beautifully crafted the plant borders may be, a simple green carpet of turf will give a depth of color and texture unsurpassed by either. An expanse of grass unites the many drifting elements of the garden, stitching them together like the pieces of a patterned quilt and creating neutral voids between color schemes and themes. In winter it creates the only significant area of green in an otherwise barren, almost leafless scene. A well-maintained expanse of lawn around the middle of a garden will contribute greatly to the verdant peace and tranquility found there. A medium-sized garden that is solidly planted with fine flowering shrubs, small trees and herbaceous plants, and traversed by hard-surfaced paths and

Crocus tommasinianus
This species, in its natural straight form of slender pale sapphire-lavender flowers, is a great joy when the flowers unfurl in the first watery spring sunshine. Originating in Dalmatia, this rapidly multiplying bulb increases both by seed and bulb division, to colonize large areas quickly and efficiently. Planted with Cyclamen coum *and* Galanthus nivalis *in areas of lawn, its grass-like foliage dies away discreetly, permitting the early resumption of lawn care.*

Laying a lawn

The two methods of laying a lawn—sowing seed or laying sods of turf—each have advantages and disadvantages. Sod has the major advantage of establishing a usable surface quickly, unlike a seeded area which even after several months must be treated with care. Sod does not require a finely prepared seedbed which grass seed demands, and there is not the same danger from weed infestations, as with delicate seed mixtures. The edges to borders and drives may be instantly defined. However, sod is expensive compared with seed mixtures and demands to be laid immediately, whereas seed may be sown at your own convenience when time and weather permit. While a grass seed mixture may be tailored to your requirements, sod is difficult to obtain other than in a standard form.

In terms of preparation, the land to be sodded should first be dug to clear it of all perennial weeds and large stones. If any deep compaction has occurred, this should be broken up (see page 24) before raking the soil surface and firming it lightly by roller or by treading. Before sowing grass seed, the cleared land should be cultivated by rotovating or hand-forking. Some time should then ideally be allowed to elapse before leveling the site and finely raking it over to produce a light but firm seedbed.

The best season for establishing a lawn will depend on whether you are laying sod or sowing seed. A lawn to be sodded is best laid when sod is normally available and when there is no danger of winter damage. New grass growth commences immediately. Watering will be essential in dry weather, for eight to twelve weeks after laying. The seeded lawn must be established in more favorable months. The best solution might be to use a combination of the two methods—namely, sodding detailed edges and border surrounds and seeding the broad centers of the lawn.

Unlike paving or a loose surface such as gravel, the lawn is a living entity, changing with each season, and the way in which it is maintained will dictate its appearance. A regularly cut and rolled lawn provides a smooth, tidy carpet of green. In total contrast, the same material may be allowed to grow long and to flower in an orchard setting, before being cut and the resultant hay raked off, then to be roughly cut every two weeks. A garden comprising varying levels of lawn maintenance will have some long grass, full of native grasses with some wild flowers, giving a sea of color in early summer, in contrast to the well-groomed expanse of lawn elsewhere.

Laying sod

The cleared, weed-free site must be firm (but not compacted) and level, with a fine covering of loam to enable the young roots to grow through quickly. Lay the rectangles of turf to avoid the continuation of joints which may open up in dry weather. Position smaller pieces within the lawn, not at the outer edges. Always stand and work from a wooden plank, to avoid stepping on the soft sod. Once it is laid, tamp down the sod with a broad, heavy wooden tamper, or use a roller.

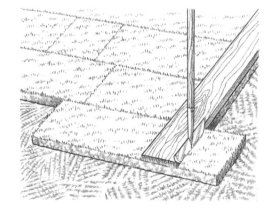

Use a board against which to cut accurate straight edges on new sod.

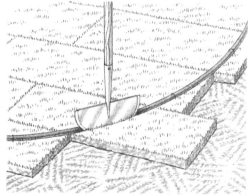

Cut a curved corner against a length of hose. A generous curve looks best.

ABOVE *Areas of well-groomed carpets of lawn certainly have their place but less manicured areas of grass can have a charm of their own in the right setting, such as around these aging pear trees. In early summer the flowering heads of grasses and wild flowers, such as clover and ox-eye daisy* (Leucanthemum vulgare), *offer a rich natural alternative to the man-made herbaceous border. In late summer the area beneath the trees should be trimmed and cleared of cut grass to ensure a fine display the following year.*

Lawn maintenance

While an area of paving or gravel may require no more than a bimonthly spot treatment of weeds with a herbicide or Dutch hoe, a lawn will demand weekly attention throughout the summer and a continuing program of regular care, to achieve weed-free, healthy grass. But modern machinery has transformed lawn maintenance, making it possible to look after significantly large areas in a short space of time. To a certain extent, the layout of the garden must adapt to the gardener and the machine, but *not* to the extent where one can recognize obvious labor-saving, machine-oriented features.

Shaping the lawn

A lawn comprising simple lines, uncluttered by physical obstacles of trees, beds of shrubs, garden furniture or wayward bulbs, with free-flowing lines and generously rounded corners, will be the easiest to maintain with a large machine. The smaller and tighter the curves and corners, and the more beset with obstacles the lawn is, the more tedious the mowing will be. If a tight corner can be widened to form a longer sweep, especially on a concave lawn curve, mowing will be easier. Access to a lawn for machinery and people should be as easy and as broad as possible to spread the wear and tear by "traffic" at specific points. Paths and narrow strips of grass should always be at least two mowers' width, to allow the mower maneuverability against the edges.

Trees set within a lawn may cast heavy shade beneath them, preventing the growth of healthy grass. These areas could be more satisfactory if redefined as borders, planted with shade-tolerant, low shrubs and perennials as far as the edge of the trees' canopy, if appropriate. Overhanging tree and shrub branches will eventually cause damage to grass edges. They should be removed back to the lawn edge, or alternatively, the grass edge cut back to a point beyond the obstruction. Bulbs should only be planted in informal areas of grass which can be left to run to seed, allowing bulb leaves to wither and die away before cutting them. It is better to plant solid areas of bulbs in dense clumps, and leave mowing in this area until later, rather than to attempt mowing through sparsely planted bulbs. A sloping lawn, which at its lowest point remains damp and impossible to drain, may be planted as a bed with moisture-loving plants to draw the water out.

Where plants are liable to droop over the edge of a planted border, a mowing edge, consisting of a hard surface such as paving stones or brick, should be laid against the lawn. This strip should be no more than 12–18 in. wide; it should preferably be constructed from a dark material, to be hidden in summer beneath plants, and to look restrained in winter, so that it is not revealed as a bright curb running through the garden. Set this strip just below the lawn surface to enable a mower to pass over it.

Where mowing edges are not used, the edge of the lawn should be kept in good order by annual cutting with a half-moon edging iron, establishing a clean line by slicing off a sliver of sod, leaving the boundary of the lawn clear of the planted border. The use of edging shears once a week, after mowing, will keep the whiskery side-growths of the lawn in trim. Any broken lawn edges may be repaired with a square of sod, cutting back into the lawn sufficiently to make a substantial insert. Always sod above the surrounding lawn to compensate for sinkage.

Lawn mowers

The style of lawn required will determine the type of lawn mower to use. For a very fine, closely cropped lawn, you will need a cylinder mower which has a series of blades mounted on a revolving drum and a roller of some weight to smooth the lawn. The more blades mounted on the drum, the finer the cut. These machines, which may be hand pushed, or driven by gasoline engines or electric motors, will put stripes of pale and dark green alternating across a lawn. Fit the mower with a box to collect trimmings.

Where a hard-wearing lawn is desired, it is necessary to leave a deeper "pile" on the lawn to withstand a greater degree of use. A mower with a rotary blade positioned horizontally over the grass, supported within a wheeled encasement, would do this. These machines have no roller, leaving the grass open in texture; they are much lighter in construction than cylinder mowers and will cut a greater variety of grass heights and conditions. They may be fitted with a grass collecting box, otherwise they will distribute the grass across the lawn to be raked up or to dry and disappear.

If lawn mowings are not collected and are allowed to accumulate on the lawn, there will be a buildup of dead material ("thatch") beneath the grass, on top of the soil. This returns some nutrients to the lawn and, in drought conditions, this thin layer of grass clippings conserves the moisture of the lawn. But in most cases it is preferable to collect the clippings and to integrate them with garden and household waste on the compost heap, where they will supply heat.

For use on grass in difficult positions, such as slopes and banks, and for under low spreading shrubs, a hover mower is useful. These have a rotating horizontal blade which is held above the ground on a cushion of air. Driven by a gasoline engine or an electric motor, they are very light to handle. They will not collect the grass trimmings.

For the larger garden, you may need a ride-on or tractor mower. These too are available with either cylinder blades or rotary blades. They may be fitted with grass-collecting devices, particularly if they are rotary models, and may also be equipped with a trailer. Ride-on machines reduce the time it takes to mow a lawn but their disadvantages are that they are expensive, heavy and poor on wet grass; on wet land, their compaction of ground can cause poor growth. You may well require a second, hand mower, to deal with the areas inaccessible to the tractor mower.

Trimmers are of great benefit to the busy gardener. They are capable of creating a fine edge to lawns or of cutting tough waist-high meadow grass where spring bulbs have died away. Used with care, they will deal with awkward edges quickly, for example, against a wall where grass has grown tightly into the stonework, or around a pond edge, or indeed any place where a mower cannot safely reach. Trimmers may be gasoline-driven, electric, or battery-powered, with nylon cord "flails" or solid nylon or steel cutting blades. They must be treated with great respect as they are highly dangerous tools and protective footwear, heavy-duty trousers and goggles should always be worn when using them.

Regular mowing alone will provide an adequate lawn of reasonable color and strength. To improve the lawn and maintain a superior standard, you need to adopt a regime of care comparable with that for a herbaceous border. The operations involved are detailed in the panel on Lawn Care, left. You will also need to carry out lawn repairs as required. Uneven surfaces can to some extent be leveled out by rolling, which also stimulates side-shooting and hence the mat-forming growth of grass. Cylinder mowers have heavy rollers built into them, but the majority of lawns cut by a rotary mower would benefit from a heavy roll in spring and then monthly rolling throughout the summer. More severe bumps must be remedied by peeling back a section of sod to shave off some soil before replacing the sod carefully. Shallow hollows in a lawn can be built up over time by sieving a fine layer of loamy soil over the depression, still letting light through, and allowing the grass to grow through before repeating.

Moss can be a problem on shady lawns, especially after a wet summer or a mild, damp winter. Scarifying in autumn (see left) will remove some moss, but doing this in conjunction with the use of a proprietary moss killer, following the manufacturer's instructions, will give better results. Take steps to improve soil drainage and to let in more light to prevent the problem from recurring.

Changes of level

A site of naturally varied levels, where steep and gentle slopes twist into a variety of contours, has itself much to offer the well-planned garden. By using the varied levels to advantage, a garden of great character may be created. Planting trees on a higher level will turn them into substantial features in a relatively short space of time. Walks or more formalized paths taking a lower route will quickly feel the weight and dominance of neighboring higher plantings, giving age and an established appearance to a comparatively young planting. Level changes can also be used as garden dividers, each level of a terraced slope forming a distinct area.

Natural level changes

In some gardens changes of levels are a fact of life, when the whole garden is on a slope. If this is too acute and awkward, it can be terraced, forming weight-supporting retaining walls, or creating a series of grass banks between the level surfaces. When using a natural change of gradient, you must balance the desire for as large a flat area as possible against the visually unattractive high retaining walls that this could necessitate. It is perhaps better to introduce a number of retained levels of narrower proportions, rather than just two, with prison-like walling and precipitous steps between them. The impact of a high retaining wall may be reduced by forming another retaining wall immediately in front of this, allowing only the width of a border between the two walls and building the second just 3 ft. or so high, filling the gap with good soil and planting. This border or foundation planting will help to reduce the visual and physical bulk of a high retaining wall significantly.

It is not always necessary to create solid, hard-looking retaining walls. Banks and slopes will provide a simpler, more natural approach at a fraction of the cost. A skilled mechanical digger operator is capable of detailed refinements and precise formal and informal contouring of soil. A crisply defined grass slope, or a curvaceous informal grass embankment, can add a delightful feature to the garden while serving a useful purpose.

When creating any change in level do take account of access needed for wheelbarrows, garden tractors and mowers, as well as any elderly or disabled visitors. Where banks are to be used, these can be grassed, preventing wear and erosion of the soil. But have your mower standing by to try out the slope of the soil before it is completed with a capping of topsoil. On a planted bank, ground-covering

Making a retaining wall

A wall which is subjected to the pressure of a weight of soil on one side must be strongly constructed to withstand this force. A double wall needs to be built on heavy, solid foundations, similar to a brick wall (see page 34). A concrete-block wall built to support the soil behind can be tied in with wire ties to a more aesthetically pleasing facing wall. A drainage pipe backfilled with coarse gravel and led off to a soakaway or ditch will carry water away and limit the problems it causes when combined with frost.

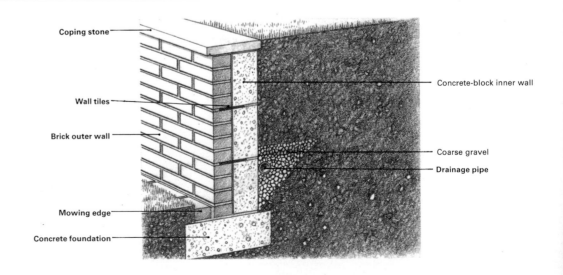

Coping stone

Wall tiles

Brick outer wall

Mowing edge

Concrete foundation

Concrete-block inner wall

Coarse gravel

Drainage pipe

plants may be used to knit the surface together quickly—plants such as *Vinca major*, *Sasa veitchii*, *Hypericum calycinum*, *Campanula glomerata*, *Alstroemeria* and *Euphorbia robbiae*, which spread by means of runners or underground stems, are ideal as their habit has the effect of stabilizing a vulnerable slope.

Creating banks

Planting on raised banks can, where necessary, form an ideal screen and sound-baffle where a new road threatens to intrude on a house and garden. The banks should, if possible, be broad and of a gentle gradient, to look as natural as possible. In some extremely wet areas, it will prove difficult and slow to establish trees and shrubs in a heavy clay soil with little good topsoil. The wet soils remain cold for longer into the spring and hence root growth is slow. Under such conditions a long-established practice is to mound-plant, by raising the natural ground level in the vicinity of the planting hole by just over 2 ft., using well-draining, loamy soil. This will give the plant a chance to put out healthy, strong roots which will then be better able to penetrate the unfavorable natural soil. Hedges in wet areas may also be planted on banks; raising them up above waterlogged fields and gardens will encourage better growth.

A raised level change—whether in the form of a simple mound or a walled, raised bed—can also provide a different growing medium to suit particular plants. Some bulbous and alpine plants require a very free-draining, poor soil, while others may need an isolated raised bed to be filled with a soil or compost of a different pH level to that of the surrounding natural soil.

Retaining walls

Retaining walls constructed to terrace a slope or to contain a raised bed should be faced in a material compatible with the garden's existing hard surfaces. Use climbing and trailing plants to break the hard edges and sides of the walls. While the walls are under construction, you can build in pipes running

through the wall and into the soil behind, to enable a scattering of plants to colonize the wall's surface once the pipes are filled with a good potting compost. Choose plants appropriate to the different aspects.

Where one wishes to deceive the eye by reducing the effect of a retaining wall or sloping bank, plants may be used to conceal at least part of the level change. Where possible, use plants in front and behind the wall or bank which in time will almost link together in places. Shrubs planted above the level change should be broadly rounded in shape to fit over the top of the retaining wall or bank—tall, slim specimens will only emphasize the increase in height. At its foot, plantings must also be rounded, billowing and capable of hugging the wall. Where banks are to be planted with trees and shrubs, I enjoy using specimens known for their tiered branching arrangement such as *Acer palmatum*, *Cornus alternifolia* 'Argentea,' *Cornus controversa* 'Variegata' or *Viburnum plicatum* 'Lanarth.' When planted on an incline they provide a gentle terrace-like impression of well-ordered levels rising up in stages.

A gentle slope in a garden may be broken into a series of strongly defined, level-surfaced lawn areas held in place by low retaining walls. The dry stone walls create a strong architectural impression in their own right, making a significant contribution to the garden's design. Predominant in the herbaceous borders are clumps of dianthus with salvias, hardy geraniums, achilleas and peonies, backed by shrubs and woodland planting beyond.

Flights of steps

A well-designed flight of steps should blend into the garden, effortlessly linking two levels which may otherwise appear disjointed and alien. The style, design and material of the steps should be influenced by the general architecture of the house and garden and should relate to the immediate area of the steps, whether they run through a retaining wall or into a bank. The scale of a flight of steps should be appropriate to its site. In a modest garden, cut-in steps may take the form of simple stone slabs supported by and run into the side of a bank; at the other extreme, in a large formal garden a freestanding flight of steps may be built with curved treads and risers, flanked by balustrade-topped walls and capped with pairs of finials at head and foot.

Both treads and risers are equally important visually. They can be, but need not be, constructed from the same materials—sometimes a contrast of color and texture makes for a more pleasing effect.

Always consider the practicalities of steps: in wet weather, stone, brick or wood-surfaced steps will become very slippery and wet steps may freeze in winter. A roughened, non-slip surface will help prevent this, but well-constructed steps should also be angled to shed water so that they dry relatively quickly. The treads of steps *must* always be securely fixed by means of mortar, as a loose tread can all too easily lead to an unpleasant accident.

The relationship between the proportions of risers and treads is all-important: if correctly calculated and executed, your normal walking pace should be uninterrupted by the passage of steps. The relationship will obviously vary with the material used and with the site, but as a general rule a riser should be between 5 in. and 9 in. in height and have a tread between 12 in. and 18 in. deep.

Materials for steps

The most effective way of integrating steps into the garden is by using materials already present within it. Using a paving slab identical to the path surfaces for the tread of the step, and a brick or reconstituted stone block similar to that used in walls for the riser, will give the steps a sense of belonging rather than the look of an afterthought. Regular steps formed from stone slabs or blocks, or from bricks laid in intricate patterns, may be appropriate in most settings, but occasionally a more unusual material or style may be called for. A path running through a densely planted area of trees and shrubs may use either wooden roundels as stepping stones, or a bark or gravel surface retained by round, rustic edging

Cut-in steps

Where space is limited or where a discreet set of steps is required, steps can be cut into a bank or retaining wall. Measure the height of the bank to work out how many steps are needed. First dig out the rough shape of the flight of steps, compacting the earth at each tread position. Dig foundations of about 10 in. for the first riser and fill with concrete (ballast and cement) over a compacted coarse gravel base. Cut in for each subsequent step before completing the previous one and fixing the paving slab in place.

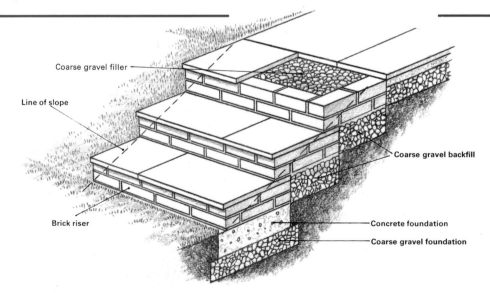

Coarse gravel filler

Line of slope

Coarse gravel backfill

Brick riser

Concrete foundation

Coarse gravel foundation

ABOVE *A generous flight of curved brick steps looks neat in a modest garden. Brick offers a good grip in wet and icy weather.*

ABOVE RIGHT *Steps formed from risers of wooden railroad ties are backfilled with coarse gravel and surfaced with gravel to form a level change.*

rails. If a level change is encountered here, rustic steps should be built, consisting of wooden risers held in place by stakes driven into the ground. The treads are made up with ballast topped off with either gravel or bark chippings to be retained by the riser. Railroad ties are often used in a modern scheme to form low retaining walls negotiating a gentle slope, perhaps with the use of gravel mulches beneath plantings. To continue this theme, the simplest of steps may be constructed using the long, broad ties to build generously wide and deep steps on a gentle incline. Avoid ties with tar- and oil-

contaminated surfaces which, in hot weather, will actively ooze from the timber for many years.

Using plants
If provision is made when constructing steps for a slip of soil to be introduced against the riser at the back of the tread, small plants may be introduced to soften the lines of the steps and link with similar plantings in the wall itself, or in borders. Another way of using plants to soften the outline of steps is to place containers at their sides, filled with a riot of scrambling and trailing summer-flowering plants.

Freestanding steps

A shallow flight of steps which rise, freestanding, from ground level to a terrace or lawn on a higher level held by a retaining wall will have greater impact. Upon a solid foundation of compacted coarse gravel and concrete, as for cut-in steps, each level is built in a brick framework to the height of the riser, and the middle cavity filled with compacted coarse gravel. The flat tread of each step should overhang the riser by 1–2 in., to shed water clear of its surface.

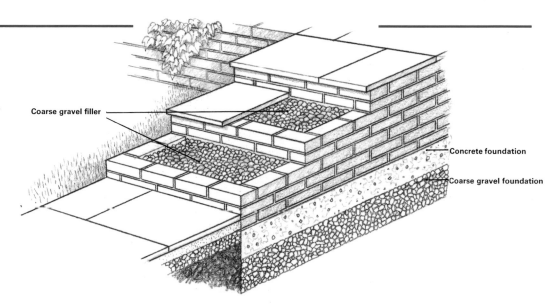

Coarse gravel filler

Concrete foundation

Coarse gravel foundation

Plantings to edge steps

Sunny, exposed steps in late summer

Symmetrical planting on either side gives strength and formality to these stone steps leading from the edge of a terrace to the lawn. A planted bank can comprise many plants requiring a free-draining soil as such areas rarely remain wet. This planting theme of blue flowers and silver-blue foliage links well-shaped plant species together at the level of each riser. The spreading growth of *Viola cornuta* and the rounded solidity of a pair of lavenders (*Lavandula angustifolia*) mark the sides of the first step. *Nepeta* and *Buglossoides* cascade on to and down the steps while *Perovskia* and *Aconitum* 'Bressingham Spire'

create height at the sides. In late summer *Agapanthus* Headbourne hybrids, with their drumstick-like flowers, mingle with the spiky leaves of *Yucca gloriosa*, leading the eye up.

1 *Aconitum* 'Bressingham Spire'
2 *Agapanthus* Headbourne hybrids
3 *Buglossoides* (syn. *Lithospermum*) *purpurocaerulea*
4 *Ceanothus* × *delileanus* 'Gloire de Versailles'
5 *Hebe* 'Pewter Dome'
6 *Lavandula angustifolia*
7 *Nepeta* 'Six Hills Giant'
8 *Perovskia* 'Blue Spire'
9 *Viola cornuta*
10 *Yucca gloriosa*

Woodland steps on a shady bank in late spring

In an informal setting of unrestrained planting a discreet, rustic set of steps is most appropriate. Half-sections of round posts supported by wooden pegs create the risers, backfilled with bark-topped ballast for the treads. Plants colonize the steps and diminish their impact. Some small plants furnish the step risers, like the fern *(Polypodium vulgare)*, Creeping Jenny *(Lysimachia nummularia)* and the carpeting plant *Soleirolia soleirolii*. Small-leaved ivies provide all-year-round cover. Low-growing plants at the sides help to

merge the steps with the bank. Other plants such as *Skimmia japonica* and the male fern *(Dryopteris filix-mas)*, although taller, will furnish themselves down to the ground. Behind these grow tall shade-loving plants like willow gentian *(Gentiana asclepiadea)*, the beautiful white-fringed campion *(Silene fimbriata)* and the brilliant blue *Cynoglossum nervosum*.

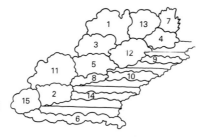

1 *Astrantia major* 'Shaggy'
2 *Cardamine trifolia*
3 *Cynoglossum nervosum*
4 *Dryopteris filix-mas*
5 *Gentiana asclepiadea*
6 *Hedera helix* 'Hazel'
7 *Iris foetidissima* 'Variegata'
8 *Lamium maculatum*
9 *Lysimachia nummularia*
10 *Polypodium vulgare*
11 *Silene fimbriata*
12 *Skimmia japonica* 'Rubella'
13 *Smyrnium perfoliatum*
14 *Soleirolia soleirolii*
15 *Uvularia grandiflora*

EMBELLISHING THE GARDEN

Ornamental and structural features are the embellishments which turn a well-planted, carefully designed garden of interest and beauty into something more. The use of well-selected features, cleverly combined with all the other elements, bestows an individual personality upon a garden, giving it a magical, atmospheric quality.

The effective juxtaposition of statuary and plant material can bring a special quality to a garden. Here an Italianate statue against a wall is half-concealed by the bold foliage of Vitis coignetiae *shrouding the wall and a pot-grown* Hydrangea macrophylla *'Ami Pasquier,' in late-summer flower above a carpet of* Viola labradorica.

Garden features

What we call garden features may take the form of buildings, sculpture and even plants, but what they have in common is their potential to ornament a garden, even when they have a functional role to perform at the same time. Garden buildings include temples, gazebos and summer houses; they should have some architectural merit, as well as providing shelter and protection as a garden "house" or room. Pergolas, arbors and arches contribute substantial weight and strength to the design of a garden, besides being host to an extended range of climbing, scrambling and twining plants.

The smaller-scale, decorative items to be found in a garden include pieces of sculpture and ornaments such as sundials, bird baths and containers. They contribute greatly to the garden's character and provide the owner with an opportunity for self-expression outside the confines of the house. Features involving water can breathe life into a still and motionless scene; wall fountains, ponds, streams or lakes each have their own charm. The use of attractively designed garden furniture will give pleasure to the eye as well as being functional. The simplest and the most natural structural features are the plants themselves. A well-placed tree or shrub shown off to maximum effect by neighboring plantings will form a simple but strong statement, as will a grouping of herbaceous plants that are architectural in outline or with bold leaves or flowers.

Siting the features

The placing of a visual highlight must be exactly right, or its impact is all but lost. A basic consideration is whether an ornamental feature should stand out as an obvious attraction, noticeable immediately as one arrives in the garden, or whether it should have a lower-key identity, well placed but waiting to be discovered. Summer houses and gazebos should obviously be placed where they will be warmed by the sun, preferably oriented to catch the late-afternoon sunshine for as long as possible and so that they are bathed in watery sunshine even on a winter's day. Aesthetic and practical points must be reviewed

and balanced against each other. A summer house or garden seat may look wonderful in a certain setting, but if it faces away from the sun, or is in the shade of large trees, then its usefulness will be limited.

Pairs of features, such as ornamental urns or topiarized trees, are a useful means of controlling a view or emphasizing a smaller feature, and they give importance to a large scheme. Never set a matching pair too far apart, otherwise they will not be viewed together. Light-colored features set amid dark surroundings will perform as though lit by a spotlight. For example, a fine wooden seat with an intricately worked, Chippendale-style back, painted cream or white, will look marvelous standing against a finely clipped evergreen hedge that is almost black in color. Avoid such a visible feature at the far end of a garden, as its eye-catching qualities will prove too distracting.

Water features

Water features take numerous shapes and forms, and whether large or small they introduce a quite different element into the garden. This element visibly moves, reflects its surroundings and creates sounds, as well as enabling us to grow different types of plants at its damp periphery and within it. Water also encourages wildlife including insects and birds as well as the fish and frogs we may introduce into it. A wall fountain, comprising a water-spouting mask and a collecting bowl or tank beneath, makes a beautiful adornment to any terrace, where the sound of water on a hot day is a calming influence. A square pool to the side of a paved terrace will provide wonderful reflections and an oasis of stillness in an otherwise busy vicinity. A well-designed pool will, in its surface area, counterbalance similar-sized areas of plantings or paving.

The formal pool or pond is generally angular and symmetrical in appearance, tidily bordered with regular, square paving stones. The informal pond is best treated as naturally as possible to link closely with the soft areas of the surrounding garden; its general shape should follow the flowing contours of

The sounds as well as the sight of running water can create a soothing effect in a garden. Here the water splashing over large pebbles in a simple trough falls from a classical lion-head mask on the wall above, framed by the prodigious growth of a hop (Humulus lupulus). *Brightly painted terra-cotta pots contain the sculptural forms of clipped box.*

the land or be of deep irregular curves. The water's edge should be planted to merge the water closely with the garden. In both cases, the higher the water level, the better the effect, both for water's reflecting qualities and to disguise unsightly lining materials. The formal pond, particularly a small one, is often constructed with vertical sides; where the water is deeper than 3 ft., provision should be made for wildlife to escape, in the form of a submerged ledge (this is also useful for placing aquatics and marginal-plant-filled baskets). The informal pond usually comprises steeply sloping sides, ideally with provision, in the form of ledges, for water plants; it should also have areas of shallow and deep water to suit different plants and species of pond life.

Making a statement

Where a collection of well-designed and carefully placed features are brought together in one area, an emphatic statement is made. Even a single element, a lone spreading tree at the far side of a lawn, will have strong bearing on the garden as a whole, perhaps indicating where the manicured part of the garden stops. Structural features can act as indicators, not just of a style or period, but also as directional signs, for example channeling someone

between a pair of pedestal-mounted urns to a final statue. This may sound grandiose, but the smallest of gardens may adopt the same principles. For example, a pair of containers on the edge of a narrow terrace may be mirrored, in design and planting, across a small lawn. These containers, shouldering an opening in a trellis screen, lead the eye to a centrally

A small enclosed herb garden is made into a special feature by means of its own focal point, the small statue on a base, and the surrounding "hummocks" of clipped box.

Making a wall fountain

The water is recirculated by means of a small electric pump, so it is necessary to have a safe outdoor electricity supply to the fountain. A separate reservoir chamber enables the cables and pipes to be hidden below ground; it also hides and soundproofs the submersible pump, provided the cover is lagged. The height of the mask is partly determined by the power of the pump, and how high it will project the water. The fountain system should be drained of water before the onset of winter to prevent any damage through freezing.

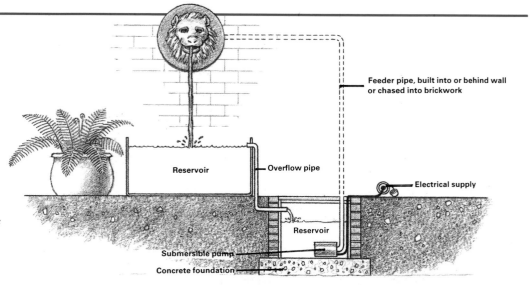

Feeder pipe, built into or behind wall or chased into brickwork

Reservoir

Overflow pipe

Electrical supply

Reservoir

Submersible pump

Concrete foundation

placed statue or urn in front of which a paved surface allows an arrangement of table and chairs. The whole could be contained within an area measuring no more than 33 ft. × 26 ft.

A piece of sculpture can humanize an area otherwise lacking any signs of man-made intervention and might be used to give added depth to a foreshortened garden. Sculpture, statues and urns make a satisfactory focal point, drawing the eye; they may act almost as a full stop to the garden, or at least provoke an exclamation mark if positioned at the far end. Plantings grown as a backdrop will enhance the feature, and at the same time help to merge ornaments with the garden. Garden seats or a pair of chairs make a less pleasing focal point: placed at the far end of a view, they are too functional to be attractive, no matter how ornamental their design. And an empty seat has a lifeless, forlorn look about it, which is not generally appealing. Benches and seats are better placed to the sides of a garden, where they may be glimpsed but are not always in view.

Creating height

Arbors, arches and pergolas may take many different forms, from the simplest structure partially supported by a house or garden wall, to large, freestanding, elegantly designed colonnades or tunnels. Their uses are varied, for they can create movement through a garden, linking different areas with one another, or they can tempt people to stay in an "outside room" where seats and shade are provided. The planted arbor, arch and pergola have sufficient height and weight to create impact in the garden, but their open structures prevent them from looking too solid. In effect they make a mental rather than a physical division between areas.

The construction of these structures should, wherever possible, take some inspiration from the surrounding buildings. If a curved arch is to be formed, this may take its lines from a house, window or door of arched-top design. With a pergola, the vertical piers may be built of timber, brick or stone, and where possible you should use a material similar to that used in the house. This is of greater importance if the pergola is to extend out from the house itself: a structure of different materials will look decidedly tagged on, if it is not integrated with the adjacent building in some way. The height of windows or the style of a carved lintel will, if carried through to the design of the pergola, link the structures. A pergola's vertical supports should always be equally and precisely spaced. When there are many of them, they form an interesting rhythm, lining a garden path or the edge of a terrace, and the shadows cast from them will increase the effect.

A series of freestanding arches has the same effect as an ironwork tunnel across a garden, except that as

PLANTS TO CLOTHE
A PERGOLA
Actinidia chinensis
  (Chinese gooseberry)
Clematis orientalis
Cobaea scandens
Humulus lupulus
  'Aureus' (golden hop)
Jasminum officinale
  (summer jasmine)
Laburnum × watereri
  'Vossii'
Lonicera japonica
  'Halliana' (honeysuckle)
Rosa 'Blush Rambler'
R. longicuspis
Schizandra rubrifolia
Vitis vinifera (grape vine)
Wisteria floribunda

Building a pergola

A secure pergola relies upon solidly positioned wooden posts, or piers of stone or brick filled with a core of concrete. (See page 42 for erecting fence posts.) Beams running the length of the pergola rest on the uprights and the cross-beams run at right angles to form the overhead superstructure; their ends overhang the supporting posts and may be attractively cut and finished. Thinner beams may cross the large cross-members, running the length of the structure; these can prove useful when securing wayward climbers.

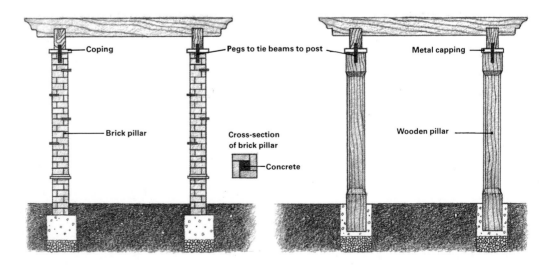

Coping

Pegs to tie beams to post

Metal capping

Brick pillar

Cross-section
of brick pillar

Concrete

Wooden pillar

the arches are not connected you can step out on either side of the covered path. Viewed from either end, however, the arches will seem to join, forming a continuous tunnel or pergola. A latticework tunnel, if well sited, will form the main axis of a garden, drawing the eye along its length to a distant focal point. If paved with brick beneath, the corridor feeling will be enhanced by the use of a running bond (see page 64). A very simple tunnel across a path may be established as a short-term measure for, say, just one summer, with the use of bamboo canes or bean poles of rustic wood bent over and tied in the middle. This will support the growth of annual climbers, such as sweet peas *(Lathyrus odoratus)* or, in a vegetable garden, runner beans.

Training climbing plants

When determining the height and width of an arch or pergola, do bear in mind that the climbing plants which are to clothe them will demand a certain amount of growing space. In wet weather you will not find it pleasant to be brushing against soaking foliage, so there should be enough width to accommodate people and plants comfortably. To allow two people to pass each other, without being pricked by rose thorns, allow a width of $6\frac{1}{2}$ ft.; in a modest-sized garden, 4 ft. is wide enough for one person. For a pergola, the concrete footings for the vertical supports need to be wider than the base of the vertical for stability and support, but they should not be too large as this is where the climbing plants are to be established. The broader the footings, the farther away the plants have to be placed.

Extra support will be required by these climbers to secure them well, for they are much more exposed than climbing plants on a solid wall. You will need to fix strand wires or fine wire mesh vertically against the uprights to provide sufficient tying-in ground (see page 38). Training deciduous climbers on a pergola designed to shade a hot terrace in summer makes an ideal sun shade, allowing only dappled sunshine through; once the climbers lose their leaves in winter, this allows in maximum light when levels are generally low. Outside the house windows, evergreen climbers that give permanent shade would prove much too dark in northern climates in winter.

ABOVE *The elaborate white-painted latticework pavilion forms a strong structural feature in this garden divided into compartments. Clad in rambling roses, it focuses the eye on the "room" beyond.*

LEFT *An untreated wooden pergola adds height to the middle of the garden and offers light support for the rose 'Rambling Rector.'*

Using plants as features

Plants with a naturally strong form are of great help to both the garden designer and the gardener, as they require little further maintenance after planting and their unpruned freedom ensures a natural shape. A plant may be selected for its architectural form, such as a yucca; its shape as a specimen tree or shrub, for example, a mulberry (*Morus nigra*); or for its fine foliage, perhaps deeply scalloped, as that of a fig (*Ficus carica*). Do not be tempted to consider flowers too highly when choosing plants as features as they are so short-lived. Look for berried plants or plants with interesting leaf and stem color as a longer-term attraction (see "Feature plants" and "Specimen trees and shrubs," pages 114–19).

Where a tree or shrub is required for impact, you will find that a clump of three or five specimens, of for example *Malus floribunda*, planted relatively close together will provide a more substantial block for immediate effect, especially if viewed from afar, whereas one wisp-like trunk would be insignificant for several years. Where shrubs are used, the full number may be left to mature into a rounded clump. An individual tree of good, shapely appearance such as *Catalpa bignonioides*, placed on a lawn or within the curve of a border, will form the most natural feature in the garden, providing an ever-changing impression through the seasons and its evolution to maturity.

Trained shapes

Trees that are tolerant of rigorous pruning and clipping can be used to produce a measured, formal impression. A line or block of clipped evergreens grown into geometric shapes or a precisely spaced run of clipped deciduous trees are good examples of using plants as part of the garden's architecture.

Pleaching and pollarding trees and the creation of stilted hedges illustrate well the practice of training plants into shapes. These forms of training use only those trees which are amenable to the tortuous shaping involved, principally linden (*Tilia*) and hornbeam (*Carpinus*), although other genera may be used such as *Malus*, *Sorbus* and *Salix*. Pleaching involves planting a line of specimens which are trained in a single plane to produce vertical trunks from which accurately spaced horizontal branches are extended to meet the branches of the neighboring tree, until they eventually join together. This system of training, which takes eight to ten years, requires the support of wires and posts (see below). Pollarding involves removing all growth back to the crown of the trunk or to shortened, arm-like branches, which promotes the vigorous growth of strong young wood and a mass of foliage. This material is cut back every year or as infrequently as every six to eight years, depending on the scale of the site and whether a formal or less formal effect is required. The creation of a stilted hedge is almost a combination of

Against a mature backing hedge of hornbeam (Carpinus betulus), additional specimens have been grown up and trained to form a stilted hedge, making a dramatic effect in a formal garden. In the green niche formed at the right angle of the hedges a classical lidded urn is raised upon a plinth, creating an effective focal point.

Pleaching trees

Extra height may be given to an existing wall or fence by the precise siting of young, straight-stemmed trees rigorously trained for pleaching. A system of equally spaced tensioned wires supported upon sturdy posts makes an ideal training frame and should be put in place after the first year. Once the structure of pleached trees is complete and sufficiently stable, after about eight years, the posts and wires are removed. Each year, in late winter, the previous season's growth is removed, leaving only the basic structure of verticals and horizontals.

1

2

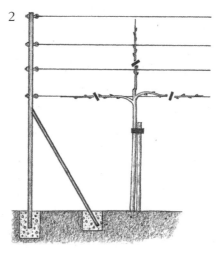

1. Young trees are set in position and tied to stakes. When they reach the desired height for the first branches, cut the terminal shoot to this level in late winter. Next spring, the shortened shoot will stimulate the top three buds: the terminal bud will grow straight up and the lower two will develop behind it.

pleaching and pollarding. The young trees again require a structure upon which to be trained, but instead of being confined to a single plane the upper branchwork is allowed to fill out to form a box-shaped head as dense as a hedge while beneath, the stilt-like legs hold the hedge aloft. Trimming the top as for a hedge will keep the structure in shape.

These three forms of training have a specific role to play when a high-level garden division is needed. Raising the height of a wall or fence may prove very costly whereas a row of pleached specimens will, without covering the surface of an attractive wall, form a screen above, where height is required, blocking off any overlooking neighbors or high vehicles and showing only a line of pillar-like trunks.

Demonstrating another form of rigid control, topiary specimens make wonderful impersonations of other structures, whether real or imaginary. Simple geometric shapes are usually more satisfactory than those of peacocks or teddy bears. Where the shape requires sharp angles to be produced on corners and across the top, the play of light and shade will make them come to life. The use of evergreen shapes will be particularly welcome on bleak winter days, when they are sharply defined against frost or snow.

Holly *(Ilex)*, yew *(Taxus)* and box *(Buxus)* form ideal evergreen topiary as their relatively small leaves may be clipped to a fine surface. This is a slow process requiring great patience because the best

topiary is that which is dense, tightly grown and hence slow to form into shapes. When creating a new shape, a wire frame or former may be placed over the unclipped young specimen and the plant then clipped to this shape; this can be purchased or home-made from fine-gauge wire. But with time and a good eye, most shapes can be gradually formed with the use of sharp pruning shears and hand pruners. Start out with a full, bushy plant which will offer the greatest potential for shaping. These plants require only one trim in late summer, although a second in late spring will create a tighter form.

Topiary may also be used in containers to give strong winter shapes. Containers planted with attractive flowering compositions for spring or summer add character to a garden and are of greatest benefit on a terrace or area of the garden that is used a lot. But every situation is potentially a container site —tailoring the planting to the aspect is the gardener's skill. One large pot is generally more satisfactory than a large group of smaller ones; three pots of graduated sizes grouped together can produce a pleasing effect, but try to use just one style and material within a grouping. An urn or pot that is attractive in its own right is further enhanced by an equally appealing planting. Pairs of containers planted identically are pleasing in their symmetrical formality, especially where they are used to emphasize an entrance or flight of steps.

SMALL TREES FOR
A SMALL GARDEN
Amelanchier lamarckii
Crataegus laevigata
  'Plena'
Cydonia oblonga
Gleditsia triacanthos
  'Rubylace'
Malus floribunda
Mespilus germanica
Morus nigra
Prunus × subhirtella
  'Autumnalis'
Pyrus calleryana
  'Chanticleer'
P. nivalis
Salix purpurea 'Pendula'

2. *When these lower shoots have extended and while still supple, tie them down to the first wire. Tie the terminal shoot to the wire above. The next late winter, prune the side branches to just beyond a bud, removing half the current annual growth. Prune the terminal shoot to the second wire to begin the process again.*

3. *When the desired height is reached, remove the terminal shoot and lead the final tier out along the wires. The current year's growth of the lateral "arms" is shortened back by half each year to promote a well-furnished leafy framework. The laterals of neighboring trees will eventually graft themselves together.*

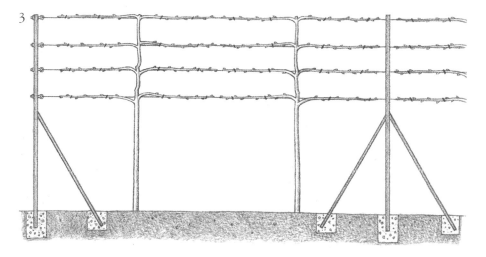

Plant-clad garden features

Ironwork arch in midsummer

A simple metal-framed structure spanning a path frames an entrance to a new area of the garden. It must be well clothed with vigorous climbers to create an entire arch of greenery. The well-pruned *Wisteria floribunda* trained to the right side of the arch will give a dramatic display of freely hanging, exceptionally long racemes in early summer. *Clematis* 'Perle d'Azur' makes a good combination with the wisteria's pale leaves, once the wisteria has finished flowering, against which its large washed-out blue flowers look attractive. *Rosa* 'Sanders White,' a rambler, will make ample growth to cover fully the left side of the arch, displaying its pure white flowers. Providing a late studding of white star-like flowers, *Solanum jasminoides* 'Album' delicately winds its way into the rose.

Shade-giving pergola in late summer

A freestanding pergola built to provide shade will require extensive planting to justify its size. The wooden structure should be well clad, which may entail planting two or more climbers of different characteristics on some uprights. Here a woody plant, *Rosa longicuspis*, is combined with *Clematis* 'Jackmanii Superba' and sweet-smelling honeysuckle with *Clematis flammula*. This provides an extended season of interest, with more flower color, and "fleshes out" the whole structure with lush growth. Climbers of a dense habit such as the jasmine and *Clematis rehderiana* are better planted alone on one upright. *Solanum crispum* 'Glasnevin' will display a sprinkling of flowers from midsummer into early autumn. The purple-leaved vine will give interest even when wet weather has ruined all the flowers of rose and clematis.

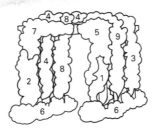

1 *Clematis flammula*
2 *Clematis* 'Jackmanii Superba'
3 *Clematis rehderiana*
4 *Jasminum officinale* 'Variegatum'
5 *Lonicera periclymenum* 'Graham Thomas'
6 *Nepeta* 'Six Hills Giant'
7 *Rosa longicuspis*
8 *Solanum crispum* 'Glasnevin'
9 *Vitis vinifera* 'Purpurea'

Garden seat in midsummer

This well-placed seat flanked by borders is set against a yew hedge and surrounded by sweet-smelling plants. A narrow strip of paving beneath forms an all-weather surface; tightly ground-hugging thymes placed in crevices in the paving release a pungent scent whenever crushed. A pair of rosemary plants flanks the approach to the seat followed by lavender and common sage. The sweetly scented foliage of *Rosa eglanteria* carries its rich scent on warm, damp evenings. In early summer *Philadelphus coronarius* will overpoweringly scent the air, to

be followed at midsummer by the perfume of *Buddleia alternifolia*. Fennel gives off a licorice scent, especially when crushed or bruised. The annuals *Lathyrus odorus* and *Nicotiana sylvestris* each give their own perfumes to combine with the intense scent of *Matthiola incana*.

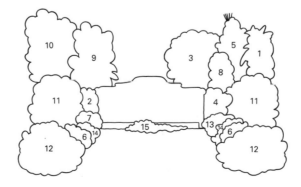

1 *Buddleia alternifolia*
2 *Dictamnus albus purpureus*
3 *Foeniculum vulgare*
4 *Geranium macrorrhizum*
5 *Lathyrus odoratus*
6 *Lavandula angustifolia*
7 *Matthiola incana*
8 *Nepeta sibirica*
9 *Nicotiana sylvestris*
10 *Philadelphus coronarius*
11 *Rosa eglanteria*
12 *Rosmarinus officinalis*
13 *Ruta graveolens* 'Jackman's Blue'
14 *Salvia officinalis*
15 *Thymus vulgaris*

THROUGH
THE SEASONS

The garden is an ever-changing kaleidoscope of color and form, varying greatly from one season to another and from one year to the next. The continuing and flourishing development of the well-planned garden relies upon a seasonal program of tasks, involving the care and control of plants and the maintenance of the garden's general fabric.

The strong, structural elements of this garden are impressive even in the depths of winter. The dark evergreen yews (Taxus), clipped holly (Ilex) and deciduous beech hedges (Fagus), covered in a light dusting of frost, provide a contrast of shapes, forms and color, while the garden furnishings of containers, seats and obelisk frames do much to lessen the sense of winter desolation.

Winter

Winter need not be bleak in the garden. Small-leaved, traditional evergreens such as box (*Buxus sempervirens*) are attractive whether clipped and shaped or left unclipped. Hedges of box and yew (*Taxus baccata*) take on the angular precision of brick walls in winter while ivies (*Hedera*) look lustrous, with hints of bronze and purple. Holly (*Ilex*) and Portuguese laurel (*Prunus lusitanica*) will also give distinctive form to the garden, with their variety of leaf shapes and color. Plants that flower in winter are particularly special. Christmas box (*Sarcococca*) produces small, white, heavily scented flowers in midwinter. In late winter, mahonias display excellent foliage and form combined with richly fragrant flowers.

Winter is the time to tackle tasks that would be impossible in other seasons. Large, established plants can be moved with the least risk since they are dormant and will not dry out. Renovation work, such as resurfacing a gravel path, can also be contemplated.

Maintenance

- In fine weather, paint or treat any exposed woodwork or ironwork. Use preservatives that are not harmful to plants.
- Have the lawn mower serviced.
- Reshape trees, shrubs and large climbing plants. Prune the previous year's growth of apple trees to a finely branched structure. Spray all fruit trees with a tar-oil winter wash on a fine midwinter day when the growth buds are tight and still dormant. Attend to pleached and pollarded trees (see pages 98–9).
- Prune roses once the weather improves and danger from frost damage is passed. Remove dead and diseased wood, also weak and congested growth. As a general rule, take off two or three older shoots to stimulate new growth from the base. Shorten flowered shoots to

The bright red young stems of *Cornus alba* seen against dark evergreen conifers bring winter interest to a garden.

induce new shoots and flower buds.

- Cut back wisterias and vines, whose annual growth was reduced by half in midsummer, to two buds beyond last summer's growth, except where you want the plant to spread.
- Prune and shape late-summer-flowering shrubs, such as hydrangeas, buddleias, *Perovskia* and *Caryopteris*.
- Prune *Clematis* species and cultivars that flower from summer to autumn on growth produced in the current season. Remove all growth above the lowest pair of strong buds. Large-flowered clematis hybrids also benefit from a winter prune to reduce the length of the previous season's growth by half and to allow flowering before the summer pruning.
- Use a rubber rake or besom broom to brush over lawns to disperse worm casts.
- Clear garden corners of wayward leaves. Check that you are not depriving hibernating animals of their homes—in spring they rid the garden of pests such as slugs and snails.

- When temperatures do not rise above freezing, tie burlap or even old sheets around containers and ornaments made of soft porous stone or terra-cotta, even if they are frostproof.
- In midwinter, especially when very low temperatures are forecast, wrap the trunks of tender shrubs with burlap or netting to prevent frost from penetrating the bark.
- Knock heavy coverings of snow off the boughs of trees and shrubs.

Larger projects

- This is the time to take out an old hedge to make way for existing, half-grown replacements or plant a new one. Cut a trench on either side of the hedge, using an axe to cut through any large, extended roots, and work the old hedge plants loose.
- Remove any shrubs and small trees that may have outgrown their site or which are in decline due to old age. Take off the head of a small tree at shoulder height, leaving a sturdy trunk to act as a lever. Dig a large enough surrounding trench to stand in, then lever out the small tree or shrub, working from underneath.
- In drier weather, roughly dig over empty borders and new borders to allow the rain and frost to break the soil down to a fine tillage. Incorporate bulky organic material, such as compost or rotted manure, at the same time.
- Remove the surfaces of gravel paths that have become muddied and, as a result, weed-infested, by scraping off the gravel layer with a shovel, then redressing with new material. Use the gravel "sweepings," minus the weeds, to improve drainage, especially on heavy, clay soils; dig them in with organic matter to a depth of about 12 in.
- Remove growths of lichen, algae and moss from paving. A high-pressure hose will remove most of the growth but spraying or painting with tar-oil wash, according to the manufacturer's instructions, should remove it all.

Spring

The strong lines of the garden in winter are now rapidly softened by the growth of plants. Paving edges and the hard corners of walls are broken by ground cover or climbing plants. Crown imperials *(Fritillaria imperialis)* nose their way through the warming soil, releasing their strong scent from unopening leaves. Catkins on suckering hazel clumps are fully extended, showering clouds of pollen at their small, red female flowers. The early pea *(Lathyrus vernus)* throws up bushy mounds of growth studded with pink and purple flowers, complementing the fading blooms of *Helleborus orientalis*. Biennials, such as Scotch thistle *(Onopordum acanthium)*, evening primrose *(Oenothera biennis)*, *Silybum marianum*, foxglove *(Digitalis purpurea)* and mullein *(Verbascum olympicum)*, break dormancy, sending out attractive basal leaves.

Lawns will begin to knit back together after standing dormant and wet through the winter, and areas that were earlier full of narcissi, crocuses and anemones will run to seed quickly; do not mow until the foliage has died down. In the borders other bulbs are appearing, such as alliums with their globes of purple, mauve or occasionally white or yellow, and camassias, with their spire-like heads of blue or cream starry flowers.

By late spring, a wealth of flowering shrubs will have burst forth into a dazzling array of color, marking the end of clear, fresh, spring tones of predominantly yellow and green. Lilac *(Syringa vulgaris)* is one such shrub which, when mature, will put on a great show of flowers for several weeks.

The warmer weather makes spring a good time to undertake any constructional projects. For example, you might wish to consider laying or relaying paving, the repair of retaining walls or, in early spring, the final preparation and laying of sod.

Spring cherry blossom (Prunus 'Kanzan') *with the brilliant young leaf color and white flowers of* Pieris *enlivens a simple courtyard.*

Maintenance

• Apply long-term preventive herbicides, following the manufacturer's instructions, to prevent weed infestations on paths and drives during the growing season.

• In early spring, cut down shrubs such as dogwood *(Cornus alba)* and willow *(Salix alba)*, which are grown for their colored stems, to a "stool" just above ground level, allowing two buds of the current year's growth. This will promote strong, well-colored growth for the following winter. This should be practiced every two or three years.

• Prune and shape early-flowering shrubs such as forsythia, winter jasmine *(Jasminum nudiflorum)* and flowering currant *(Ribes)*. Remove some of the flowered material but retain the plant's overall shape.

• Give permanently planted shrub and herbaceous borders a dressing of balanced fertilizer to add a boost of nutrients at a time of rapid growth and ideal growing conditions. Scatter

and leave it, or fork it in.

• Spread a thick carpeting mulch of organic matter over permanently planted flower borders when the soil is moist.

• Support tall and weak-stemmed herbaceous perennials such as delphiniums early in their growth with brushwood, canes and string or metal supports. Make sure they are loose enough to allow further growth.

• Toward the end of spring, if time permits, trim box topiary back into shape. This will keep the growth tight and dense. Trim them again in late summer (see page 99).

• As young shoots of clematis rapidly expand, prevent them from running into each other by opening out the growth and tying the separate shoots into place. Do the same for golden hops *(Humulus lupulus* 'Aureus'), honeysuckle *(Lonicera)*, everlasting sweet peas *(Lathyrus)* and any other soft shoots on fast-growing climbers.

Larger projects

• Remove any remaining loosened mortar and replace the jointing of walls and paving that have lost their defining, mortared joints over the winter (see pages 36 and 68).

• Spring is a busy time for lawn maintenance. The first cuts made should just top the grass off; the edges must be re-trimmed with a half-moon edging iron; broken edges and bare patches should be re-sodded or seeded. Start feeding, weeding and killing the moss in the lawn, particularly in showery, damp conditions. Irrigate the lawn in late spring if the weather has been dry. From the end of spring you will need to mow the lawn regularly, perhaps twice a week (see page 85).

• Climbing plants will need to be encouraged to grow in the right direction through their supporting wires, trellis or mesh. Rapid young growth made in this season can easily be damaged by wind and rain so regular tying in with soft twine is important (see page 38).

Summer

Trees are now re-clothed in pale green foliage; even the walnut (*Juglans*) and mulberry (*Morus*) will break reluctantly out of dormancy to cover their naked branches. Deciduous hedges that form only light, semi-permeable screens during the winter are transformed into the most solid of barriers, totally altering the scale, perspective and even sounds within the garden.

Arbors, pergolas and trellis all but disappear beneath luxuriant growth. Walls and fences become lush barriers of great textural quality. Herbaceous borders burgeon with plants such as *Acanthus*, *Delphinium* and *Crambe*, jostling for space while sprawling plants at the front of borders begin to flow out over paving, gravel or edging slabs. Well-tended pots will now be bursting with summer-flowering plants such as *Verbena*, *Diascia*, *Argyranthemum* and *Pelargonium*. The flamboyance of summer is hailed by the unashamedly violently colored and blowsy Oriental poppies (*Papaver orientale*). Always place poppies well back in a border, as they begin to wither very early in the summer season. The fast-growing, early-flowering Banksian rose (*Rosa banksiae* 'Lutea') produces its clusters of small, pale yellow flowers.

Maintenance

● Spray roses every two weeks, from early summer through to autumn, to prevent infestations of aphids and attacks by mildew and blackspot. Follow the manufacturer's instructions carefully. An initial spray after pruning in early spring will ensure they are clean at the start of the growing season. Add a few drops of a liquid detergent to help ensure that the insecticide adheres to the aphids.

● Give a twice monthly liquid feed to all containers full of plants. Shrubs, herbaceous plants and even young trees can also be promoted into stronger, healthier growth by liquid feeding.

Sunlight pierces the open canopy of a black mulberry tree (Morus nigra) *in high summer, casting dappled shade on the hammocks.*

● Any trees carrying dead limbs can be dealt with by a tree surgeon at this time of year.

● Mow lawns, twice a week in damp, warm conditions, and continue weeding them, using a selective weedkiller, and feeding them with sulfate of ammonia.

● Remove the dying flowerheads from plants, except those with attractive seedheads such as poppies, alliums and roses with hips.

● Secure the sappy, long growth of strong-growing climbing plants, at least temporarily, otherwise it can easily be damaged and lost to summer storms. Climbing roses, *Solanum*, vines and *Rubus* all need careful handling. When securing any collapsed growth, position it only once, then tie it securely.

● Check the existing ties on fast-growing wall shrubs, climbers and trees. In this season the girth of young trees that are staked and tied will expand rapidly and ties that are too tight can cut into the fast-expanding main stems.

● Continue to stake tall herbaceous perennials.

● Remove the over-ripe seed heads of plants which distribute their seeds rather too freely.

● Prune *Clematis* species and cultivars which have flowered in the spring on the previous year's growth, for example *C. alpina*, *C. macropetala* and *C. montana*. Cut back the flowered laterals to within two to three buds of the original framework as soon as the flowers have faded to avoid damaging the emergent new growth. Very vigorous species may be carefully pruned with shears to remove excessive growth rather than allowing them to become a tangled mass. Those large-flowered clematis hybrids pruned in winter should, when flowered, be pruned again to reduce the total number of shoots. This will encourage the shortened stems to produce a new framework, so replacing the whole framework over a number of years. Young growth produced from mid- to late summer pruning will often provide an autumn flush of flowers.

Larger projects

● In spells of extreme or prolonged heat and drought, watering of flower borders becomes increasingly important. Use irrigation hoses that dribble water over their entire length through small perforations. These are far more effective than overhead sprinklers.

● Vigorous climbing plants such as fruiting grapevines and wisteria demand summer pruning. Reduce the length of the current season's growth by approximately a half to three-quarters in midsummer, to allow air and light to reach the main plant.

● Prune early-flowering shrubs, including *Philadelphus*, *Deutzia*, *Kolkwitzia* and *Weigela*, immediately after the petals start to fall. Remove a third of the oldest material to make way for, and encourage, young, strong, growth from the base of the plant. Remove any dead or damaged wood and any weak growth at the same time.

Autumn

This transitional season is notable for its extremes. Some of the hottest and driest days of the year may be experienced in the early part of autumn, but heavy rain or frost may be commonplace at the other end of the season. Autumn marks the beginning of the season when plants may safely be moved again. Even when the autumn rains do come, the soil is still warm from the summer and capable of promoting new root growth before the onset of the winter and a long period of dormancy.

Toward the end of autumn much new nursery stock becomes available and there is no better time for the planting of trees and shrubs. Planted in the autumn, shrub roses, hedging plants, specimen trees or fruit trees will have the advantage of winter rains, followed by an encouraging spring to set them off to a flying start. If you order plants by mail order, open their boxes and check them immediately after they arrive and water them; if wrapped in damp newspaper, unwrap them. If you cannot plant straightaway, then heel the plants into a border or put them together in large pots of soil or potting mixture in a sheltered position until planting. Very small plants, on the other hand, should first be potted and then placed in a cold frame or cold greenhouse until they have produced more roots and grown big enough to be ready for planting out in the garden.

Autumn need not be an anti-climax after summer. Leaf and berry colors can be as eye-catching as flowers at this time of year. Many species of mountain ash *(Sorbus)* and crab apple *(Malus)*, remarkable for their flowers earlier in the year, are ready with a final curtain call, showing off dramatic fruits, particularly *Sorbus* 'Joseph Rock' and *Malus* 'Red Sentinel.' For leaf color, the thorn *(Crataegus lavallei)* provides a good display of red, coupled with clusters of orange berries which are retained throughout

A wall-trained pear (Pyrus) *puts on a dazzling autumnal display of russet leaves against weathered brick.*

winter. The service berry *(Amelanchier lamarckii)* has crimson fruit, ripening to deep red, while its leaves turn orange and then red. Some climbing plants, such as *Pyracantha*, *Cotoneaster, Celastrus, Actinidia deliciosa* and *Vitis coignetiae*, will brighten fences, walls and the house itself with their attractive fruits.

Maintenance

• Start raking up leaves early in the season. Add them to the compost heap or stack them separately to rot down as leaf mold. Beech and oak make the best leaf mold—avoid chestnut and sycamore, which are slow to rot. Lay fine netting across border and ponds to facilitate the speedy removal of leaves.

• Plant hardy bulbs as early as possible to prevent dehydration.

• Remove tender summer bedding from containers, potting up any permanent plants. Plant with appropriately scaled hardy evergreens, as well as bulbs and bedding, for the spring.

• Make sure the supporting structures for climbing plants are secure and sufficiently strong for the increased size of the plants they support, before the onset of winter.

• Plant evergreen trees and shrubs in mid- to late autumn. Some may need the protection of a roll of fine-mesh plastic or burlap around them to see their susceptible evergreen growth safely through their first winter and to prevent the desiccating effect of late winter winds. Support the plastic or burlap on a wigwam of canes to keep it free of the plant.

• Protect deciduous plants of doubtful hardiness by making a tent of burlap-covered bamboo canes to place over the whole plant if small, or make a sleeve of burlap to wrap around the base of larger plants. Coir (coconut-fiber) spread over the base of delicate plants will assist their passage through winter.

• Topiary of box *(Buxus sempervirens)* should have its main annual trim in early autumn to reinstate the desired shape. If it had been trimmed in early summer, it should need only a light tidying up now.

• Order sufficient quantities of organic matter for the winter digging ahead—ideally, use farmyard manure, otherwise mushroom compost or spent hops.

Larger projects

• Remove at least a third of the soft green wood of large roses that are looking top-heavy to avoid wind damage over the winter.

• Check the strength of tree stakes and ties on young trees to prevent casualties during autumn gales and high winds.

• Carry out lawn repairs using sod or seed to correct bumps and hollows and repair any damaged lawn edges (see page 84). All lawns should be raked to remove dead grass, aerated by spiking, and top-dressed with a loam-based brand-name medium. In mid-autumn, lawns may be laid using a seed mixture or sod.

KEY PLANTS FOR THE WELL-PLANNED GARDEN

At the risk of omitting some trusted treasures, I have limited myself here to selecting plants whose virtues are numerous and whose applications are extensive. I give at least equal importance to foliage as to flowers since most plants will be in flower for only two to three weeks a year, whereas finely marked or deeply toothed, bold or delicate leaves, for example, will give pleasure for the entire summer—or throughout the year if they are evergreen.

A fine classical balustrade is draped with the long, elegant racemes of Wisteria floribunda 'Alba.' The wisteria's twisting growth has been allowed to weave its way in and around the balusters. Even when not in flower, the attractive pale green compound leaves and extravagant growth of the wisteria enhance garden walls or architectural features; in winter its rough silver-gray bark is of ornamental interest.

Individually, all the plants mentioned here will make fine specimens, worthy of inclusion in any well-planned garden. In the majority of cases I have listed plants which help to link hard and soft areas, contributing strong, architectural lines to the essentially rigid lines of beds or lawns, or bringing a softening influence to hard expanses, such as paving or boundary walls. Always remember that the art of good planting lies in combining plants that complement and enhance one another, drawing out the finer qualities of each individual. On a more practical level, plants should be of a compatible size, height and growth rate to neighboring plantings if they are to live in harmony with one another. They must also be suited to the environment into which they are planted. For example, an *Abutilon suntense* may promise a most exciting partnership with a particular color strain of *Primula japonica* but neither would survive for any length of time while enduring the type of soil and amount of sun needed by the other.

Crambe cordifolia

Border plants

Convolvulus elegantissimus

Convolvulus has an unfortunate reputation, gained from the pernicious bindweed species within the genus, but there are some fine species whose sprawling tendencies can help to pull a border together. *C. elegantissimus* is one of the most beautiful; if suited to soil and site, it will colonize a border, spreading by underground shoots. Emerging in spring, its tight, silvery shoots expand rapidly to form deeply scalloped, silver-green leaves. As with other *Convolvulus*, the quickly extending shoots coil around any unsuspecting host. Flower buds are produced like twists of candy wrappers, unfurling to display strong, sugary pink funnels, startling in their clarity of color, throughout summer. Planted with bronze-leaved plants, the silvery growths of *Convolvulus* stitch the planting together and enliven the foliage with colorful flowers.

Size H: to 4 ft.; S: to 6 ft. in 2 years. **Aspect** Full sun. **Hardiness** Variable; requires some protection. **Soil** Free-draining, light, warm. **Planting partners** *Salvia officinalis* 'Purpurascens,' *Rosa glauca*, *Berberis thunbergii* 'Rose Glow,' *Hebe pinguifolia* 'Pagei.'

Crambe cordifolia
(Kale)

There are few herbaceous plants which can rival the dynamic, dramatic growth of *C. cordifolia*. It appears as if from nowhere in mid-spring and within a few weeks large plain leaves are stretching over the bare soil. Its

small, well-spaced flowers open a pure white, with greenish-yellow centers, in early summer. The cloud-like quality of the flowers enables one to see through them and beyond, like a veil, and makes it possible to use such a large plant in the front half of a border. **Soil** H: to 7 ft.; S: to 5 ft. **Aspect** Full sun. **Hardiness** Hardy. **Soil** Well drained, fertile. **Planting partners** Blue delphiniums, mauve *Thalictrum aquilegiifolium*, *Onopordum acanthium*, *Verbena bonariensis*.

Eryngium giganteum
(Sea holly)

Eryngium giganteum is a biennial which freely distributes its seeds; on a gravel area or paved terrace they find their way into the narrowest of cracks and will germinate and thrive, reveling in the fast-draining medium. Its attractive, silvery, thistle-like flower spikes persist through summer and into autumn, when rain finally browns the stems. Planted under peonies, lupins, delphiniums or shrub roses in a border, they make a magnificent display, lightening the overall effect of the planting.

Size H: 2 ft.; S: 10 in. **Aspect** Full sun. **Hardiness** Hardy. **Soil** Well drained. **Planting partners** *Sisyrinchium striatum*, *Nepeta nervosa*, *Borago pygmaea*.

Eupatorium maculatum
'Atropurpureum'

In late summer, when many herbaceous plants are on the wane, this long-lived herbaceous perennial pro-

vides a rich, healthy high point at the back of a border. Late to emerge in spring, its tall, spear-like shoots slowly gain in height over the summer season. The flat heads of pinkish-purple open at the end of each stem and provide a great attraction for butterflies and bees. Their coloring is suitable for the end of the summer, when flower colors tend to intensify and russet tones begin to show on herbaceous peonies and knotweeds. If used in the herbaceous border, its coloring would be in harmony with other late-flowering subjects, and in the mixed border it looks good against bronze or pink-tinged foliage. On exposed sites staking may be needed, but in sheltered positions, despite its height, staking is unnecessary and detrimental to its graceful lines.
Size H: 4–5 ft.; S: 2 ft. **Aspect** Full sun to part-shade. **Hardiness** Hardy. **Soil** Well drained, deep, rich. **Planting partners** *Verbena bonariensis*, *Aster novae-angliae* 'Andenken an Alma Potschke,' *Cotinus coggygria* 'Royal Purple,' *Rosa glauca*, *Salix purpurea* 'Nancy Saunders.'

Gaura lindheimeri

There are few plants with the elegance and grace of *G. lindheimeri*, but its overriding joy is that its delicate wispy growths, decked in flowers, are produced in autumn when there is little else like it in color and form. A short-lived herbaceous perennial in all but the mildest and most free-draining sites, it produces long, fine branches clothed with willow-like leaves. The white, flushed pink, flowers are moth-

like, fluttering in the slightest breeze. If planted through the center and middle of earlier-flowering herbaceous plantings, it will give a freshness and an airy mobility late into the season.
Size H: 2½ ft.; S: 2 ft. **Aspect** Full sun. **Hardiness** Moderately hardy; its chances of survival are increased if protected with conifer branches. **Soil** Free-draining, poorer soils. **Planting partners** *Hydrangea arborescens* 'Annabelle,' *Hosta plantaginea grandiflora*, *Anemone × hybrida* 'Alba' and 'Luise Uhink,' *Nerine bowdenii*, *Colchicum speciosum album*.

Kale see *Crambe cordifolia*

Knotweed see *Persicaria*

Meadow rue see *Thalictrum*

Mullein see *Verbascum*

Paeonia
(Peony)

Tree peonies, like herbaceous peonies, are short-lived in flower, yet they do display fine foliage for the remaining summer months, their foliage and general shape making them a worthy contributor in key locations of the mixed border. The attractive compound leaves of *P. suffruticosa* forms are suffused with pinkish-red, most pronounced when the leaves are opening in early spring. *P. delavayi ludlowii* is a strongly textured plant. From its early flowering in late spring and throughout the summer, the excellent pale green foliage carries this plant right

Paeonia suffruticosa

Plants tumbling across the front of a border will greatly enhance paved areas, while those elsewhere in the border will fulfill different roles and preferably provide interest through the seasons.

through until autumn. Its stems are stronger than those of *P. suffruticosa*, which may require light staking. Grown with large, mound-forming shrub roses, both species provide a useful contrast in foliage and form.
Size H: 5–6 ft.; S: 4–5 ft. **Aspect** Full sun or part-shade. **Hardiness** Hardy, but late frosts may damage early young leaves and flower buds. **Soil** Any good garden soil. **Planting partners** with *P.. suffruticosa*: *Tulipa* 'China Pink'; with *P. delavayi ludlowii*: *Tulipa* 'West Point.'

Perovskia atriplicifolia

Papaver
(Poppy)

All poppies are short-lived, many lasting only one day, but their fleeting dash of strident color will enliven any border. Annuals such as *P. commutatum*, *P. rhoeas* and *P. somniferum* will happily self-sow themselves into other plantings; their flowers, created from the finest of tissues, are only built for the day, but there is normally a wealth of flower buds still to come to keep the performance running for at least two weeks. The Oriental poppy, *P. orientale*, is a herbaceous perennial, sporting flowers of a considerable size from early to late summer. The commonest, or most frequently seen, is the orange cultivar 'Allegro,' which is blatant in its appeal but amusing when used to shock effect with blue delphiniums and violet-blue geraniums. My own favorites, 'Avebury Crimson' and the taller 'Beauty of Livermere,' are the most startling color—brilliant red with black blotches.

Size H and S: 1½–3 ft. **Aspect** Full sun. **Hardiness** Hardy. **Soil** Free-draining, fertile. **Planting partners** with *P. orientale* 'Avebury Crimson' and 'Beauty of Livermere'; deep blue delphiniums, *Anchusa azurea* 'Lodden Royalist.'

Perovskia atriplicifolia
'Blue Spire'
(Russian sage)

This subshrub thrives in hot, dry conditions. 'Blue Spire' is the most frequently seen form, with its silvery green, tooth-edged leaves and tall, upright stems, which are covered by a silvery white down. These growths extend and branch all through summer to be covered in late summer by small, lavender-blue flowers for many weeks. The plants are pleasantly aromatic when brushed against.

Size H: 4 ft.; S: 3 ft. **Aspect** Sun. **Hardiness** Hardy. **Soil** Free-draining, poor, stony. **Planting partners** *Santolina*, *Lavandula*, *Centranthus*, *Salvia officinalis* 'Purpurascens,' *Cistus*.

Persicaria
(Knotweed)

Knotweeds are invaluable herbaceous perennial plants. All are fast-growing, although some only attain a height of 4 in, forming a mat of smothering growth, while others grow to over 6 ft. Their flower color ranges from white through shades of pink to red. *P.*

affinis 'Donald Lowndes' forms neat, ground-hugging mats and, from mid-summer to autumn, produces short spikes of pink, aging to red, flowers, no taller than 6 in. *P. amplexicaulis* 'Atrosanguinea' forms a much branched plant, some 4 ft. tall, with very small crimson flowers from late summer through to autumn. *P. bistorta* 'Superba' is a fine plant, flowering in early summer upon slender stems above a basal mound of lush leaves. The 3 ft. tall "pokers" are capped with a spike of tiny bright pink flowers produced over many weeks.

Aspect Best planted in cool, part-shade. **Hardiness** Generally hardy; *P. affinis* may suffer some dieback in extreme winters. **Soil** Damp; *P. affinis* will grow on a dry bank or border. **Planting partners** with *P. bistorta* 'Superba': *Digitalis purpurea*, pink and mauve *Aquilegia*, alliums such as *Allium aflatunense* 'Purple Sensation,' *A. christophii*, *A. cyaneum*.

Poppy see *Papaver*

Salvia sclarea turkestanica

This biennial is a marvelous plant by any standard but particularly good for providing solid bulk in the herbaceous border where so much else appears thin and stemmy. With its pale mauve and white flowers, shown off against pink and white bracts, plants provide a harmonious color scheme in mid-summer. When bruised, plants give off an unpleasant smell so they are best

planted in the middle of a border or another position where you are unlikely to brush against them.
Size H and S: 3 ft. **Aspect** Full sun. **Hardiness** Very hard winters can damage over-wintering rosettes, so protect with netting or straw. **Soil** Reasonably free-draining, fertile. **Planting partners** *Campanula lactiflora*, *Delphinium*, *Nepeta sibirica*, *Rosa* 'Fantin Latour.'

Sea holly see *Eryngium giganteum*

Thalictrum

(Meadow rue)

Meadow rues can make an important contribution to any border where height is required. The muted shades of their leaves and flowers fit them to most color schemes. *T. aquilegiifolium* produces a basal clump of attractive, gray-green leaves in early spring from which rise branched stems, reaching a height of 4 ft., surmounted by heads of fluffy mauve or lilac in early summer. *T. flavum glaucum* grows from a basal cluster of pewter-gray leaves and stems grow to 5 ft. The fluffy, pale sulfur-yellow flowers are massed together.

Aspect Sun or part-shade. **Hardiness** Hardy. **Soil** Any reasonable garden soil. **Planting partners** with *T. aquilegiifolium*: *Sambucus nigra* 'Purpurea,' *Berberis thunbergii* 'Atropurpurea,' *Cotinus coggygria* 'Royal Purple,' *Foeniculum vulgare* 'Purpureum,' *Clematis recta* 'Purpurea'; with *T. flavum glaucum*: *Aconitum*, blue delphiniums, *Euphorbia characias wulfenii*, *Bupleurum fruticosa*.

Verbascum

(Mullein)

The fine seed of *Verbascum* finds its way into the most unlikely places, providing an original and innovative planting, if an accidental one. *V. phoeniceum* is a neat, attractive biennial, its stiff upright stem reaching 3 ft.; it remains covered in small, white flowers, flushed pink on the reverse, for many weeks. *V. olympicum*, also biennial, has the added attraction of silver-felted leaves and stem. The flowering spike may reach 7 ft. and the small flowers open a soft yellow, a few at a time, over a period of several weeks.
Aspect Full sun. **Hardiness** Hardy. **Soil** Free-draining. **Planting partners** *Digitalis purpurea*, *Oenothera biennis*, *Salvia sclarea*; often best alone.

Verbena

For quantity of flower across an extended season verbenas in general are hard to equal, continuing to flower until autumn without any dead-heading. Most verbenas are low, sprawling, spreading or mound-forming plants, but some have an upright stiff appearance. The ideal location for the low-growing forms is the front of a border, where they may tumble out and across a hard surface. 'Sissinghurst' has a finely cut leaf with large, pink, sweetly scented flowers; 'Silver Anne,' a broader, scalloped-edge leaf with larger, sugary pink, sweetly scented flowers. 'Loveliness' is similar in leaf size and flower size to 'Silver Anne' but with highly scented flowers of bluish-mauve. These hybrid verbenas are

admirably suited to container cultivation. Of all the upright-growing verbenas, *V. bonariensis* is probably the finest, with its flat heads of tiny, light purple flowers which open from midsummer to autumn. The plant may grow to 5 ft. high and 3 ft. wide, seeding itself enthusiastically among other plants and between paving materials. The slender flower stems usually require no staking as they are particularly wiry and tough.
Aspect Full sun. **Hardiness** Requires some winter protection. **Soil** Free-draining. **Planting partners** with *V. bonariensis*: mauve and pink *Cosmos*, *Anemone × hybrida*, *Corylus maxima* 'Purpurea,' *Foeniculum vulgare* 'Bronze.'

Verbascum olympicum

Feature plants

Plants that have exceptional structural form make an invaluable contribution to the creation of a well-planned garden.

Acanthus

The bold, healthy foliage of *Acanthus* adds solidity and weight to any planting scheme. Flowering stems rise from the herbaceous crown of the plant to display curious-looking spikes of hooded and tongued individual flowers in mid- to late summer. *A. mollis* produces large, broad, glossy leaves that are rounded and lobed; the flowers are purple with white centers, arranged like a lupin on tall stems 4 ft. high. The shorter, glossy leaves of *A. spinosus* have jagged, sharply pointed edges. The flowers are similar to those of *A. mollis* but spiny and prickly.
Aspect Prefers direct sun. **Hardiness** Hardy. **Soil** Any good reasonable garden soil, enriched with organic matter. **Planting partners** *Monarda* 'Croftway Pink,' *Nepeta sibirica*.

Angelica archangelica

Angelica should be treated as a biennial; in its second year it grows vigorously, sending up a large, hollow-stemmed flower spike from late spring to early summer. Many small, greenish-yellow flowers are produced in late summer.
Size H: 6–8 ft.; S: 3 ft. **Aspect** Part-shade. **Hardiness** Hardy. **Soil** Moisture-retentive. **Planting partners** Best alone.

Angelica tree see *Aralia elata*

Aralia elata
(Angelica tree)

In winter, the bare branches of this shrub can look like a stag's antlers. In midsummer, frothy cream panicles of tiny flowers are produced among the terminal leaf clusters. The slower-growing cultivar 'Variegata' is beautifully marked with white.
Size H: 8–10 ft.; S: 6 ft. **Aspect** Sun or part-shade. **Hardiness** Hardy, but late spring frosts can damage early leaf growth, so protect with netting. **Soil** Any reasonable garden soil. **Planting partners** *Geranium sylvaticum album*, *Polygonatum × hybrida*, *Digitalis purpurea alba*.

Artichoke, cardoon see *Cynara*

Cynara
(Artichoke, Cardoon)

This magnificent, showy herbaceous plant must be one of the finest silver-foliage plants. It will look majestic at the back of a border, or emerging through low planting. Ridged and pale green stems bear large, prickly, thistle-like flowers of a clear blue. *C. cardunculus* displays the largest leaves in the genus with intense blue flowers which are produced on 6 ft. stems in late summer.
Aspect Full sun. **Hardiness** Needs some winter protection to safeguard over-wintering crowns. **Soil** Light but rich. **Planting partners** *Crambe cordifolia*, *Acanthus mollis*.

Euphorbia characias wulfenii
(Spurge)

This splendid shrubby evergreen is an ideal candidate for growing at the edge of a gravel path or drive, merging with a planted area, or against a house. In winter the blue-gray whorls of leaves clothe stiff, upright shoots. The flowering spike develops into a large, cylindrical head of chartreuse-green flowers. A single plant may support eight to ten of these large flower spikes —an impressive sight throughout spring and early summer. Self-seeding.
Size H and S: 3–4 ft. **Aspect** Full sun. **Hardiness** Hardy. **Soil** Free-draining. **Planting partners** *Wisteria*, *Buddleia alternifolia*.

Helleborus
(Hellebore)

Few plants will perform as well as hellebores in poor light and adverse temperatures—they are well suited for planting at the base of a sunless wall or in damp and cool sites. *H. argutifolius* is an evergreen of great structural merit with woody shoots which persist through winter, clothed in toothed, divided, leathery leaves. In late winter, flower buds at the ends of the shoots open to create a head of many-cupped, pale green flowers. The evergreen *H. foetidus* has deeply cut leaves in dark green with a hint of blue. In late winter, it produces trusses of pale green flowers which expand into large, well-spaced flowerheads and last for many months. *H. foetidus* will grow to 1½ ft. while *H. argutifolius* can reach 2½ ft.

Aspect Part- to full shade. **Hardiness** Hardy. **Soil** Any reasonable garden soil. **Planting partners** *Oemleria cerasiformis*, *Iris foetidissima* 'Variegata,' *Bergenia cordifolia*, *Narcissus* 'February Gold,' *Lathyrus vernus*.

Melianthus major

This relatively tender, exotic herbaceous perennial is primarily grown for its leaves. In late spring stout shoots push through the ground, opening to reveal beautiful sea-green leaves, toothed at the edges. In a very warm autumn, the plants will produce bright red clusters of flowers at the end of each stem. A sheltered border, ideally backed by a warm wall, will provide the necessary protection required by this sun worshipper.
Size H: 6–7 ft.; S: 5–6 ft. **Aspect** Full sun. **Hardiness** Half-hardy; benefits from protection with bracken fern, burlap, straw or conifer branches in winter. **Soil** Rich, light. **Planting partners** *Nepeta sibirica* 'Souvenir d'André Chaudron,' *Atriplex halimus*, *Bupleurum fruticosum*.

Onopordum acanthium

Use giant onopordums to make magnificent, statuesque statements through a border or to create a focal point in the garden. The biennial *O. acanthium* is easily grown from seed sown in late spring. It forms a large, flattened, silvery-white rosette which hugs the ground tightly; felt-like hairs cover the huge, sharply spined leaves. From late spring onward, the plant spreads out vast silver, almost white,

leaves across the ground before pushing up a column of white-felted branches, topped with torches of bright blue to lilac flowers. Once flowered, the plant sets seed in thistle-down nests, prolonging its beauty into late summer.
Size H: 6–8 ft.; S: 3–4 ft. **Aspect** Full sun. **Hardiness** Hardy if grown on poorer soil. **Soil** Free-draining, not enriched by organic matter. **Planting partners** *Crambe cordifolia*, *Althaea rosea rubra*, *Sambucus nigra purpurea*, *Rosa* 'Rambling Rector' or *Rosa soulieana*.

Ornamental rhubarb
see *Rheum palmatum*

Rheum palmatum
(Ornamental rhubarb)

The large, simple leaves of ornamental rhubarb give great relief to borders but they also sprout elegant flower stems which reach considerable heights in early summer. 'Atrosanguineum' is grown for its coloring. When the crowns break into growth, the distorted young leaves are a rich, deep rose-purple; this coloring persists on the reverse of the leaves, while on the upper surface it is lost to a deep green. The flower spires are furnished with minute bright red flowers.
Size H: 6 ft.; S: 5 ft. **Aspect** Part-shade, shelter. **Hardiness** Hardy. **Soil** Moist, rich. **Planting partners** *Ligularia dentata* 'Othello,' *Rosa glauca*, *Rhus typhina* 'Laciniata,' *Filipendula rubra* 'Venusta.'

Helleborus argutifolius

Spurge see *Euphorbia characias wulfenii*

Yucca

The yucca is an ideal architectural plant, with its evergreen, sword-like leaves that look impressive all year. *Y. gloriosa* and its forms are the finest yuccas but site them carefully as the stiff, pointed leaves are quite capable of inflicting painful injury on the unwary. It flowers dramatically in late summer, the flower shoot measuring up to 8 ft. in height, but all too rarely. *Y. gloriosa* 'Variegata' has attractive stripes down its leaves, but is less hardy than the species.
Aspect Direct sun, ideally near a warm wall. **Hardiness** Half-hardy. **Soil** Free-draining. **Planting partners** *Hebe* 'Pewter Dome,' *H. rakaiensis*, *Stipa gigantea*, *Helictotrichon sempervirens*, *Helichrysum petiolare*.

Specimen trees and shrubs

Daphne × burkwoodii

Choisya ternata
(Mexican orange blossom)

This evergreen has a pleasantly rounded natural shape, furnishing itself to the ground with glossy green leaves, making it an ideal candidate for the front of a shrubbery or as a wall shrub grown at the foot of a climber-clad wall or fence. Unlike many shrubs, it will grow well in a sunny or shady aspect. The foliage is strongly aromatic when brushed past or crushed, releasing a strong citrus scent. During late spring and early summer trusses of pure white, sweetly scented flowers decorate the shrub. *Choisya* is very amenable to pruning, preferably after flowering.

Size H: 5–6 ft.; S: 4–5 ft. **Aspect** Sun or shade. **Hardiness** Hardy, but when young worth protecting the soft growth for the first two winters. **Soil** Any reasonable garden soil. **Planting partners** *Hydrangea anomala petiolaris*, *Hosta* 'Thomas Hogg' or 'Francee.'

Cornus
(Dogwood)

This large genus covers many plants of diverse shape and appeal. *C. alba* and its many forms, which can grow to 5 ft., are grown primarily for their colored stems in winter. 'Sibirica' is crimson-red; 'Kesselringii' has the most striking stems of deep purple, almost black; 'Spaethii' also has reddish stems, but is grown mainly for its boldly marked, gold and green leaves. 'Elegantissima' is elegantly beautiful, its white-margined leaves giving light and refinement to any planting. *C. mas*, the cornelian cherry, slowly grows into a densely branched tree with a maximum height of 20 ft. In mid- to late winter, its naked branches are sprinkled with clusters of small, bright yellow flowers, which are followed by bright, red, edible, cherry-like fruits. The green leaves turn reddish-purple before falling in autumn. The excellent cultivar 'Variegata' has attractively variegated leaves with clear green and white markings. **Aspect** Open, light, sheltered. **Hardiness** Hardy. **Soil** Moist but free-draining, rich. **Planting partners** with *C. alba* 'Spaethii': *Populus alba* 'Richardii,' *Sambucus racemosa* 'Plumosa Aurea,' *Lonicera nitida* 'Baggesen's Gold'; with *C. alba* 'Elegantissima': *Hydrangea arborescens* 'Annabelle,' *Hosta plantaginea* 'Grandiflora,' *Clematis* 'Alba Luxurians'; with *C. mas*: *Narcissus* 'Peeping Tom,' *Helleborus foetidus*, *Hedera helix* 'Arborescens.'

Crab apple see ***Malus floribunda***

Daphne

For fragrance of flower, Daphnes are in a class of their own, often almost overpowering, and their diminutive stature makes them ideal where a small permanent shrub is required. *D. × burkwoodii* 'Somerset' will grow quite quickly to a height of 3 ft.; it is semi-evergreen, particularly in a favorable site. In early summer, the branches are covered with richly fragrant, pale pink flowers. *D. odora* opens its first, reddish-purple flowers in late winter and continues into late spring; it will grow to a height of 4–5 ft. 'Aureomarginata' is a strong grower and possibly hardier than the species; the leaves are edged in a creamy white border.

Aspect Full sun to part-shade. **Hardiness** May require some protection in the first two winters. **Soil** Light, free-draining. **Planting partners** with *D. × burkwoodii* 'Somerset': *Cistus* 'Silver Pink,' *Hebe* 'Red Edge,' *Euphorbia × martinii*, *Ruta* 'Jackman's Blue'; with *D. odora*: *Euphorbia robbiae*, *Hebe rakaiensis*, *Sarcococca humilis*.

Dogwood see ***Cornus***

Elder see ***Sambucus nigra***

Juglans
(Walnut)

The walnut is a stately, majestic tree, with a wide, spreading crown of heavy branches, ideal as a large specimen within a lawn. The widespread crown and open leaf formation provide dappled sunlight, allowing grass to persist

through summer and partial shade-loving plants to thrive at its feet. *J. nigra*, the black walnut, is a fast-growing, large tree, with deeply furrowed bark and large, dark green leaves. *J. regia*, the common walnut, is a slower-growing, medium-sized to large tree. The attractive gray bark is relatively smooth save for wide, deep cracks. When fully open, the leaves are a healthy olive-green.
Size H: 80–100 ft.; S: 30–40 ft. **Aspect** Open, away from frosts. **Hardiness** Hardy, apart from late frosts. **Soil** Deep, well-drained, rich.

Malus floribunda
(Japanese crab apple)
There are few small trees more beautiful than the crab apple when in full flower and its scent is one of the most delicious in the garden. An elegant tree, it is almost pendulous in shape as it carries long arching branches almost to the ground. Generally round-headed, it is often broader than it is high. The classic apple blossom flowers open in mid-spring from crimson bead-like buds into flowers of white or pale blush-pink. Small red and yellow fruits are produced later in the summer.
Size H: 13–16 ft.; S: 15–16 ft. **Aspect** Full sun or part-shade. **Hardiness** Hardy. **Soil** Any reasonable garden soil. **Planting partners** *Narcissus poeticus recurvus.*

Mexican orange blossom
see ***Choisya ternata***

Mock orange see ***Philadelphus***

Morus nigra
(Black mulberry)
The mulberry makes an ideal specimen tree for the smaller garden since it takes on age and character quickly. It is slightly ornamental and yet small and quiet enough not to jar with subtle plantings. It forms a particularly long-lived, architectural tree, often with crooked trunk and heavy boughs. It comes into leaf in late spring; the large, rough-surfaced leaves are heart-shaped. Insignificant flowers are followed in late summer with large, edible, raspberry-like fruits, almost black in color when ripe. In autumn the leaves turn a clear yellow before falling.
Size H: 10–13 ft.; S: 13–16 ft. **Aspect** Full sun or part-shade. **Hardiness** Hardy. **Soil** Any reasonable garden soil—the richer the soil, the finer the growth. **Planting partners** *Anemone × fulgens*, *Camassia cusickii*, *Nectaroscordum* 'Siculum.'

Mulberry see ***Morus nigra***

Oemleria cerasiformis
(Oso berry)
In the coldest weather, this short, suckering shrub begins fattening its conspicuous buds which then burst into soft growth of pale green leaves, not damaged even by severe frosts. Flower buds then expand and open, resembling small chains of white flowers. If planted where it can spread

Malus floribunda

Trees and shrubs form the principal furnishing of the garden, influencing its style and atmosphere and creating shelter and shade.

by its underground suckers, a fringe-like effect may be achieved at the edge of a lawn or border.
Size H: 6½–8 ft.; S: 6½ ft. **Aspect** Sun or part-shade. **Hardiness** Hardy. **Soil** Any reasonable garden soil. **Planting partners** *Helleborus orientalis*, *H. foetidus*, *Galanthus*, *Aconitum*, *Eranthus*, *Crocus tommasinianus.*

Ornamental pear see ***Pyrus***

Oso berry see
Oemleria cerasiformis

Sambucus nigra
'Guincho Purple'

Parrotia persica

Parrotia persica makes a large shrub or medium-sized, low-branching tree; it grows slowly but steadily, producing broad, spreading horizontal boughs. Old, mature specimens have an interesting bark which sheds in flakes to give an attractive mottled pattern of different colors. In mid- to late summer, the large, deep green leaves at the tips of the branches become flushed with a bronze coloring. This marks the beginning of a long period of brilliant autumn tints. In winter short spurs on all the naked branches are clustered with flowers which appear as tufts of crimson stamens.

Size H and S: 16–26 ft. **Aspect** Full sun or part-shade. **Hardiness** Hardy. **Soil** Any reasonable garden soil, but colors best in autumn in a rich, deep soil; lime-tolerant. **Planting partners** *Crocus sativus*, *C. tommasinianus*, *Arum italicum* 'Pictum,' *Lathyrus rotundifolia*, *Clematis* 'Jackmanii Superba.'

Philadelphus coronarius
(Mock orange)

The intoxicating scent of *Philadelphus* wafting across a garden on a warm, humid evening marks the first few weeks of legitimate summer. *P. coronarius* forms a strong-growing medium- to large-sized shrub. The flowers open against the fresh, green leaves, which are the perfect foil for the creamy white, richly scented trusses. Plant it as a specimen plant backed by linden and beech trees for an impressive combination; it may also easily play host to climbing plants such as clematis.

Size H: 20 ft.; S: 6½ ft. **Aspect** Full sun or part-shade. **Hardiness** Hardy. **Soil** Any reasonable garden soil. **Planting partners** *Digitalis purpurea*, *Clematis*, climbing roses.

Pyrus
(Ornamental pear)

Where a small, formal, ornamental tree is required to give height in a small-scale garden, the genus *Pyrus* has much to offer. The early spring blossom is white with dark stamens and is followed by small fruit later in the year. *P. calleryana* 'Chanticleer' grows to 10 ft. and has a narrow pyramidal shape, making it ideal to use in a confined space or as sentinels at either side of an entrance. Its shiny, pale green leaves produce flushes of new growth in summer and its pure white spring blossom is followed by sporadic bursts of blossom throughout summer. In autumn, the leaves turn from green, through red, to maroon, clinging to the branches until late into the winter, sometimes remaining almost evergreen. *P. nivalis*, the snow pear, is a very beautiful, medium-sized tree, growing to 20 ft. tall; it is pyramidal in shape, with ascending branches which make a broad crown. Its shape is ideal for gardens of a formal layout. In early spring, clusters of pure white flowers open with the newly emerging young leaves of an intense silver. On aging, these leaves appear pale green with silvery-white cobwebbing across their surface.

Aspect Full sun. **Hardiness** Hardy. **Soil** Any reasonable garden soil. **Planting partners** *Clematis viticella* 'Purpurea Plena Elegans,' *Rosa* 'Veilchenblau,' *Vitis vinifera* 'Purpurea.'

Rosa eglanteria
(Sweet brier)

This rose is similar in many respects to the wild dog rose *(Rosa canina)*, but it has one major distinguishing factor, its scent. There is not only a perfume emanating from its fleeting flowers, but a rich scent from its leaves. For maximum foliage scent, prune or clip the plant to encourage young shoots. The fruity scent is particularly strong in spring and early summer. The plant's growth is vigorous and the strong stems are well furnished with fearsome prickles, as are the undersides of the serrated-edged leaves. In early summer, small, blush-pink and yellow-stamened flowers open. These are followed by many rich red fruits or hips which remain on the plant until the early winter.

Size H: 7–12 ft.; S: 6–8 ft. **Aspect** Full sun or part-shade. **Hardiness** Hardy. **Soil** Any reasonable garden soil. **Planting partner** *Lathyrus grandiflorus*.

Sambucus nigra
(Elder)

This hardy, fast-growing, large shrub makes an ideal screening plant, outgrowing most other hardy permanent shrubs. As it will tolerate a certain amount of shade, it can be used to fill gaps beneath large trees where privacy has been lost. It will also grow on very poor soil, even if it is thin and alkaline. It displays ornamental leaves, some attractively colored, and produces small, creamy white flowers, which are headily scented, in early to midsummer; in some cases these are followed by heavy trusses of shiny, deep purple, bead-like fruits, of great ornamental value in autumn. All forms have a rugged and fissured bark, even when comparatively young. The leaves of 'Laciniata,' the fern-leaved elder, are a lacy filigree; 'Purpurea' is a vigorous plant with deep purple leaves. As the summer advances and the heat increases, the purple becomes less solid to reveal the underlying green. The flowers are white, tinged with purple.

Size H: 16 ft.; S: 13 ft. **Aspect** Full sun or deep shade. **Hardiness** Hardy. **Soil** Any reasonable garden soil. **Planting partners** with *S. nigra* 'Purpurea': *Rosa glauca, Lavatera* 'Burgundy Wine,' *Atriplex hortensis, Salvia officinalis* 'Purpurascens.'

Snowball tree see
Viburnum opulus 'Roseum'

Sweet brier see *Rosa eglanteria*

Ulmus × hollandica
'Jacqueline Hillier'

This unusual dwarf "elm" has an unusually refined form of growth. A deciduous small- to medium-sized shrub, it has a very dense shape and in winter resembles the bones of a fish, so precisely placed are the fine branches. In summer, the branches are clothed with small, rich green, serrated-edged leaves, also precisely positioned.

Size H: 6–8 ft.; S: 3–5 ft. **Aspect** Full sun or part-shade. **Hardiness** Hardy when mature. **Soil** Any reasonable garden soil. **Planting partners** *Tanacetum vulgare* 'Crispum,' *Polypodium vulgare, Hedera helix* 'Sagittifolia.'

Viburnum opulus
'Roseum'
(Snowball tree)

This large, vigorous shrub may be grown either as a standard or be left in a more natural shape to make a handsome specimen shrub, clothed to the ground. Infrequent, random pruning will maintain a fine shape ideal for an informal area of long meadow-like grass. In early spring, small flower buds appear, developing into pale green, pendulous spheres. In early summer, they fill out into creamy white "snowballs."

Size H: 8–10 ft.; S: 8 ft. **Aspect** Full sun or part-shade. **Hardiness** Hardy. **Soil** Any reasonable garden soil. **Planting partners** *Anthriscus sylvestris, Rosa* 'Nevada,' *Syringa vulgaris* 'Madame Lemoine,' *Crataegus laevigata* 'Plena.'

Walnut see *Juglans*

Viburnum opulus 'Roseum'

Climbing plants and wall shrubs

Hydrangea anomala petiolaris

True climbers support themselves by tendrils, suckers, barbed or thorned leaves and shoots, or by twisting, spiraling stems. Wall shrubs are trained and tied in, and held back against a hard surface.

Actinidia deliciosa
(Chinese gooseberry, Kiwi fruit)
This extremely vigorous climber has a dramatic appearance with its strong, stout shoots and leaf petioles covered in dense, red hairs, and large, heart-shaped, pale green leaves, measuring up to 8 in. across. The long growths climb by spiraling around other shoots, wires or strings. A single year's growth for a maturing plant may be 8 ft. In late summer, clusters of creamy white, sweetly scented flowers with bright yellow stamens appear.

Size H: 30 ft.; S: 13 ft. **Aspect** Full sun or part-shade. **Hardiness** Generally hardy. **Soil** Light, well drained, rich. **Planting partners** *Akebia quinata*, *Wisteria floribunda*.

Cathedral bells, Cup and saucer flower see *Cobaea scandens*

Chinese gooseberry
see *Actinidia deliciosa*

Clematis
This large genus includes many diverse, but without exception, beautiful flowering plants. Because of their prodigious growth, the popular *C. montana* and its forms, which can grow to 25 ft., are best planted where they can roam freely. Cascades of small flowers, ranging from deep pink to pure white depending on the cultivar, are produced in late spring. The large, flat and rounded flowers of *C.* 'Perle d'Azur' are pale lavender-blue, produced in quantity in midsummer. 'Abundance' blooms in late summer, displaying a cloud of small, pale mauve-purple flowers. 'Alba Luxurians' has small, white flowers, marked with green.
Size H and S: 10–12 ft. **Aspect** Full sun or partial shade. **Hardiness** Hardy. **Soil** Any humus-rich, free-draining garden soil; will thrive on alkaline soils. **Planting partners** with *C. montana*: plant into fruit trees; with *C.* 'Perle d'Azur,' 'Abundance' and 'Alba Luxurians': *Ceanothus*, *Syringa*, *Philadelphus*.

Climbing hydrangea see *Hydrangea anomala petiolaris*

Cobaea scandens
(Cathedral bells, Cup and saucer flower)
This tender annual climber is useful when new walls or fences are being furnished with more permanent, but slow-growing, climbing plants. Very fine tendrils enable this plant to scale considerable heights. Its general growth is truly scandent, falling like paper chains on reaching the upper limit of its support. The large, bell-like flowers, produced in late summer, are dusky purple or blue, sometimes green, fading to white.
Size H: 13–16 ft.; S: 10–13 ft. **Aspect** Full sun. **Hardiness** Tender. **Soil** Any well-drained, enriched with organic matter. **Planting partners** *Ipomoea tricolor* 'Heavenly Blue,' *Campsis radicans*.

Everlasting pea see *Lathyrus*

Golden hop
see *Humulus lupulus* 'Aureus'

Hedera
(Ivy)

There are few plants capable of fulfilling the variety of roles that ivies satisfy. They will often grow where no other plant, including grass, would be happy, beneath trees in deep shade for example. The self-clinging aerial roots ensure a secure fixture onto walls and tree trunks alike. When ivy becomes too heavy and dominating, it can be drastically reduced by pruning and will grow back satisfactorily. It will not only tolerate low light levels and exposure to extremes of cold, but also withstand atmospheric pollution. The maturing plant will begin to produce small, pale green flowers, followed in autumn by large, dark, nearly black, fruits. The common ivy, *H. helix*, is one of the hardiest species and extremely variable within its forms. 'Glacier' has small, blue-green leaves with subtle, creamy variegation; 'Sagittifolia' and its variegated form have a pronounced five-lobed leaf. *H. colchica* and *H. canariensis* have larger, but less hardy, foliage than *H. helix*. **Size** H and S: 10–13 ft. **Aspect** Full sun to deep shade. **Hardiness** Hardy. **Soil** Any reasonable garden soil. **Planting partners** *Hydrangea paniculata*, *Cotoneaster horizontalis*, *Lonicera japonica*.

Honeysuckle see *Lonicera*

Humulus lupulus
'Aureus'
(Golden hop)

This ornamental herbaceous perennial is capable of climbing to considerable heights with its roughened, twining stems. In winter, the entire plant dies to below ground level, to re-emerge the following spring. The large, three- or five-lobed leaves are deeply toothed and a soft golden-yellow. Adequate climbing space must be provided for the hop but do not let it clamber up other plants as it is too smothering.

Size H: 13–16 ft.; S: 8–12 ft. **Aspect** Full sun or part-shade, where the leaves will take on a lime-green color. **Hardiness** Hardy. **Soil** Any reasonable garden soil. **Planting partners** *Clematis orientalis*, *Eccremocarpus scaber aurantiacus*, *Lonicera nitida* 'Baggesen's Gold.'

Hydrangea anomala petiolaris
(Climbing hydrangea)

Hydrangea petiolaris will grow well in the cool, damp shade of an unfavorable wall or on the trunk of a large tree. In spring, the pale green leaves open, turning a rich, dark green and, in autumn, they turn a clear yellow before falling. The greenish-white lacecap flowers are produced in early summer. Affixing itself by aerial roots, this vigorous, deciduous climber will make an ideal frame for other smaller climbing plants, such as clematis. **Size** H: 60–80 ft.; S: 33–49 ft. **Aspect** Light to deep shade. **Hardiness** Hardy. **Soil** Any reasonable, moisture-retentive garden soil. **Planting partners** *Clematis flammula*, *C.* 'Alba Luxurians,' *Tropaeolum speciosum*, *Hosta fortunei* 'Francee.'

Ivy see *Hedera*

Jasminum
(Jasmine)

Jasminum nudiflorum, the winter jasmine, is a hardy, tolerant shrub, producing bright yellow, star-like flowers in the middle of winter. It will grow to

Cobaea scandens

a height of 15 ft. and may spread across a wall or fence 13 ft. or more in width. Its growth needs to be tied in to wires, trellis or mesh, as it has no physical means of supporting itself. *J. officinale*, the summer jasmine, is a strong-growing, twining climber, also needing support, with a growth shape of billowing opulence. The leaves are small and divided and the clusters of flowers, produced from early to late summer, are pure white. These are delicately but deliciously scented, especially in the damp evening air. It can grow to a height of 30 ft. with a spread of 10 ft.

Aspect *J. nudiflorum*: any; *J. officinale*: sunny and warm. **Hardiness** *J. nudiflorum*: hardy; *J. officinale*: moderately hardy but tender in severe winters. **Soil** Any reasonable, well-drained garden soil. **Planting partners** with *J. nudiflorum*: *Ilex × altaclerensis* 'Golden King,' *Magnolia grandiflora*; with *J. officinale*: *Clematis armandii*, *Rosa banksiae* 'Lutea.'

Lathyrus grandiflorus

Kiwi fruit see *Actinidia deliciosa*

Lathyrus
(Everlasting pea)

The perennial climbing peas are used to greatest effect when allowed to scramble up other woody frameworked climbers or tall shrubs, using their tendrils to gain a secure hold on their host. *L. latifolius* has coarse, winged stems and flowers that vary in color from deep rose-purple to pure white in late summer. It grows from a central clump each year, whereas *L. grandiflorus*, with its large, handsome, purple flowers in early summer, spreads alarmingly via a system of underground shoots, which must be kept in check. *L. rotundifolius* has small, rose-pink flowers in midsummer.

Size H: 6½ ft.; S: 4 ft. **Aspect** Full sun or part-shade. **Hardiness** Hardy. **Soil** Any reasonable garden soil. **Planting partners** *Rosa* 'Constance Spry,' *R.* 'Zéphirine Drouhin,' *Berberis × ottawensis purpurea*.

Lonicera
(Honeysuckle)

The powerful scent of honeysuckle is part of the early-summer ambience of the garden. Honeysuckles seem to enjoy having their roots in a cool, damp position and their tops in part-shade. The long, twining growths are decked with pairs of often glaucous green leaves and long, funnel-shaped flowers. All honeysuckles require some form of structure in which to twine. *L. japonica* is a rampant species of evergreen or semi-evergreen tendency, growing to a height of 20–30 ft. The small, fragrant flowers, produced continuously from early summer through to autumn, appear white, then age to yellow. 'Halliana,' with its fine evergreen foliage, is an excellent screening subject, growing to a height of 20–30 ft. with a spread of 8–10 ft. *L. periclymenum*, the common wild honeysuckle, or "woodbine," has the richest of scents emanating from long, tubular flowers of creamy yellow through to richest red, depending upon the culti-

var. A mass of flowers is produced in terminal clusters from early summer. It will reach a height of 15 ft. and a spread of 5–6½ ft.

Aspect Part-shade. **Hardiness** Hardy. **Soil** Moist, enriched by organic matter. **Planting partners** *Clematis montana grandiflora*, *Wisteria sinensis*, *Akebia quinata*.

Magnolia grandiflora

This handsome, evergreen, large shrub or small tree, unsurpassed for its glossy winter foliage, is a classical feature of southern gardens. Free-standing, it creates a spreading, rounded-topped specimen tree. The single, open flowers, produced in late summer, are large—up to 10 in. in diameter —creamy white and deliciously scented, reminiscent of lemons. Each flower lasts for just a day or two. The excellent cultivar 'Exmouth' displays particularly large, richly scented flowers.

Size H: 20 ft.; S: 15 ft. **Aspect** Warm, sunny wall. **Hardiness** Hardy, in a warm situation. **Soil** Preferably neutral or acid; grown on an alkaline soil, the soil must be deep, fertile and enriched with organic matter. **Planting partners** *Rosa banksiae* 'Lutea,' *Cobaea scandens*.

Solanum

Solanums are ideal subjects for a warm wall in a favorable, sheltered garden, where they will grow into spectacular climbing plants in a short space of time. Their growth is scrambling so they require support and careful tying in throughout the summer. *S. crispum* 'Glasnevin,' the Chilean potato tree, is a very vigorous, semi-evergreen scrambling shrub which will reach a height of 13–20 ft. The rich bluish-purple flowers, with a bright yellow cluster of stamens in the center, are borne freely from mid- to late summer. The luxuriance of growth dictates a large growing area, making this an ideal screening plant. *S. jasminoides* 'Album' is another rapidly climbing plant, with more refined growth which has a tendency to twine; it will grow to 20–30 ft. in height. This form bears clusters of pure white flowers with bright yellow stamens from midsummer through to the first frosts of winter. It has a greater requirement for a warm sheltered wall or corner as it can, in hard winters, be reduced or killed outright.

Aspect Sheltered position in full sun. **Hardiness** Generally hardy but may require protection in severe winters. **Soil** Any reasonable garden soil, preferably alkaline. **Planting partners** with *S. crispum* 'Glasnevin': *Clematis tangutica*, *Cytisus battandieri*; with *S. jasminoides* 'Album': *Wisteria floribunda*, *Ceanothus* 'Autumnal Blue.'

Vitis coignetiae

This bold-leaved vine makes a most spectacular climbing plant. Grown principally for its impressive rounded leaves, which can measure as much as 1 ft. in diameter, this plant's general appearance is dramatic. It supports itself with strong twining tendrils; planted against a large wall, the plant will rapidly cover an entire surface, then stream back down in ribbons of growth, disguising and camouflaging admirably for the summer months. On opening in spring, the leaves and shoots are a strong, rich red to purple, which changes rapidly to a deep healthy green. In autumn, the leaves turn a startling crimson and scarlet before falling.

Size H: In excess of 30 ft.; S: in excess of 20 ft. **Hardiness** Hardy. **Soil** Any reasonable garden soil. **Planting partners** *Campsis radicans*, *Taxus baccata*.

Wisteria

Wisteria must be one of the most dramatic sights in the garden when in bloom. The small, fragrant, pea-like flowers hang in long chains, falling clear of the pale green leaves. These deciduous woody climbers are long-lived, developing silvery, roughened tree-like trunks when mature. Their almost feathery growth softens the lines of any building structure. The young stems climb by means of twining. *W. sinensis*, Chinese wisteria, is a free-flowering plant producing racemes of heavily scented, mauve flowers in great profusion in early summer. Given the space, it can climb to 60–100 ft. and is capable of scaling trees as well as walls and fences. *W. floribunda*, Japanese wisteria, is perhaps the more elegant cousin of *W. sinensis*; although shy to flower, it bears finer, longer racemes of slightly scented flowers of pale bluish-purple in early summer and its leaves are more slender. Flowering at the same time, its cultivar 'Macrobotrys' produces very long racemes, 1½–3 ft. Whereas *W. sinensis* makes a good wall climber, *W. floribunda* is better suited to a pergola framework, where its long flowers can fall freely.

Size H: 60–100 ft.; S: 50–60 ft. **Aspect** Sun or part-shade. **Hardiness** Hardy, but early flower and leaf buds can be damaged by late frosts. **Soil** Any reasonable garden soil of adequate depth. **Planting partners** *Clematis* 'Perle d'Azur,' *Vitis*, *Ceanothus*.

Vitis coignetiae

Index

Page numbers in *italics* refer to illustrations; numbers in **bold** to the chapter on Key Plants.

Abutilon
A. × *suntense* 39 (8–10)
wall protection 38
Acaena 71, 77
A. 'Blue Haze' *68* (5–8)
Acanthus **114**
A. *mollis* **114** (6–9)
A. *spinosus 79*, **114 (6–9)**
Acer
A. *campestre see* Field maple
A. *palmatum* 87 (5–8)
Acid soils, plants 18
Aconitum 113, 117
A. 'Bressingham Spire' *90* (5–8)
Actinidia deliciosa see Chinese gooseberry
Aesculus hippocastanum 81 (4–7)
Agapanthus
A. Headbourne hybrids *90* (7–11)
Ailanthus altissima see Tree of heaven
Akebia quinata 45, 120, 122 (4–8)
Alchemilla mollis 13, 14, 31, 80 (4–7)
Alkaline soils, plants 18
Allium 78
A. *aflatunense 79*, 112 (4–8)
A. *christophii* 112 (4–8)
A. *cyaneum* 112 (6–9)
Alnus incana 50 (3–6)
Alstroemeria 87
Althaea rosea rubra 115 (3–9)
Alyssum saxatile 73 (4–7)
Amelanchier 81
A. *lamarckii 99* (3–8)
Anchusa azurea 112 (3–8)
Anemone
A. × *fulgens* 117 (7–9)
A. × *hybrida 38*, 111, 113 (5–8)
Angelica archangelica **114** (4–9)
Angelica tree (*Aralia elata*) 81, **114** (4–9)
Anthriscus sylvestris 119 (5–9)
Apricot (*Prunus armeniaca*) 39 (7–9)
Aquilegia 112
Aralia elata see Angelica tree
Arbors 96
Arches *28, 29*, 96–7, *100*
Armeria maritima 63 (4–7)
Artemisia 71
A. *arborescens 79* (5–9)

A. *camphorata 74* (7–9)
A. 'Powis Castle' 71 (5–8)
Artichoke (*Cynara*)
C. *cardunculus* **114**, (6–8)
Arum italicum 118 (6–9)
Aspect, walls 38–9
Asphalt 65
Aster novae-angliae 111 (5–8)
Astrantia major 91 (4–7)
Atriplex
A. *halimus* 115 (7–9)
A. *hortensis 78, 79*, 119 (annual)
Aucuba japonica 81 (7–9)
Autumn, garden maintenance 107

Bamboo (*Sinarundinaria nitida*) *54* (6–9)
Banks 86, 87
Bark chippings
laying 69
paving materials 64
Base, paving 67, *67*
Basketweave pattern, paving *64*
Bay (*Laurus nobilis*) 49 (8–10)
Beech (*Fagus*) 103
F. *sylvatica* 48, 50, *51* (5–7)
Belgian blocks 65
Berberis
B. × *ottawensis purpurea* 122 (5–8)
B. *thunbergii 55*, 110, 113 (5–8)
Bergenia
B. *cordifolia 70*, 115 (4–8)
'Silberlicht' *41* (3–8)
Betula utilis jacquemontii 81 (5–7)
Black mulberry (*Morus nigra*) 81, 98, 99, **117** (5–9)
Blackthorn (*Prunus spinosa*) 50 (5–8)
Borago pygmaea 110 (7–9)
Border plants **110–13**
Borders, planning 14
Boundaries
establishment 30–1
fences 42–7
hedges 48–52
imaginative designs 31
planning 14
vertical dimension 27–57
walls 33–41
Bowers 29
Box (*Buxus*) 49, 50, 99
B. *sempervirens* 48, *70*, 81 (6–8)
Brachyglottis grayi 57, 77 (9–10)
Brassica oleracea see

Ornamental cabbages
Brick pavers 64, 68
Bricks
paths 76, *76*
paving 63, *63*, 64, 68
steps *89*
terraces *73, 74*
walling materials 33
walls, construction 36
Buddleia 13
B. *alternifolia 101*, 114 (5–9)
B. 'White Cloud' *4* (5–9)
Buglossoides purpurocaerulea 90 (6–8)
Bupleurum fruticosum 45, 113, 115 (7–10)
Buxus see Box

Camassia cusickii 117 (5–8)
Campanula 14, 78
C. *glomerata* 87 (3–8)
C. *lactiflora* 113 (4–8)
C. *latiloba 79* (4–8)
Campsis radicans 120, 123 (5–9)
Capping, walls 36–7
Capping rails 45
Cardamine trifolia 91 (5–8)
Cardoon (*Cynara*) **114** (6–8)
Carpenteria californica 32 (8–9)
Carpinus betulus see Hornbeam
Caryopteris × *clandonensis 41*,

74 (5–9)
Catalpa bignonioides 15, 98 (5–9)
Cathedral bells (*Cobaea scandens*) 39, *54*, 96, **120**, *121*, 122 (9–11)
Catmint (*Nepeta*) *9, 14, 90, 100*
N. *camphorata 74* (8–9)
N. *nervosa 79*, 110 (5–9)
N. *sibirica 101*, 113, 114, 115 (3–9)
N. 'Six Hills Giant' *9*, *90* (5–9)
Ceanothus 7, 120, 123
C. *arboreus* 39 (9–10)
C. 'Autumnal Blue' 123 (8–10)
C. 'Cascade' *7* (8–10)
C. × *delileanus 90* (7–10)
C. *impressus* 45, *46* (8–10)
Centranthus 18, 112
C. *ruber 57*, 77 (4–9)
Cercis siliquastrum see Judas tree (6–8)
Chaenomeles speciosa see Quince
Chamomile nobile 77 (6–9)
Cherry laurel (*Prunus laurocerasus*) 49, 54 (7–9)
Chimonanthus praecox see Winter sweet
Chinese gooseberry (*Actinidia chinensis/A. deliciosa*) *9, 47*,

96, **120** (8–9)
Choisya ternata see Mexican orange blossom
Chrysanthemum maximum 63 (5–8)
Cimicifuga racemosa 78 (4–8)
Cistus 71, 112, 116
C. *purpureus 79* (7–9)
C. 'Silver Pink' 71, 116 (7–9)
Clematis 38, 45, **120**
'Alba Luxurians' 116 (5–8)
C. *alpina* 106 (4–9)
C. *armandii 74*, 121 (7–9)
C. *flammula 100*, 121 (6–9)
'Jackmanii Superba' 118 (4–9)
C. *macropetala* 106 (6–9)
C. *montana 54*, **120** (6–9)
C. *montana grandiflora* 122 (6–9)
'Nelly Moser' *28* (4–8)
C. *orientalis 96*, 121 (6–9)
'Perle d'Azur' *100*, 123 (4–8)
C. *recta* 113 (4–8)
C. *rehderiana 100* (6–9)
C. *tangutica* 123 (3–8)
C. *viticella* 118 (4–9)
Climate, site assessment 17–18
Climbing hydrangea (*Hydrangea anomala petiolaris*) 39, *40*, 116, *120*, *121* (5–8)
Climbing plants 97, **120–3**

Plant hardiness zones

This hardiness map will help you to establish which plants are most suitable for your garden. **The zones 1–11 are based on the average annual minimum temperature for each zone and appear after the plant entry in the index.** The lower number indicates the northernmost zone in which the plant can survive the winter and the higher number the most southerly area in which it will perform consistently.

ZONE 1	BELOW −50° F
ZONE 2	−50° TO −40°
ZONE 3	−40° TO −30°
ZONE 4	−30° TO −20°
ZONE 5	−20° TO −10°
ZONE 6	−10° TO 0°
ZONE 7	0° TO 10°
ZONE 8	10° TO 20°
ZONE 9	20° TO 30°
ZONE 10	30° TO 40°
ZONE 11	ABOVE 40°

dry stone walls *41*
walls 38–9, *38*
Climbing roses *27, 28, 33,* 45, 118
Clipping, hedges 48, 52
Cobaea scandens see Cathedral bells; Cup and saucer flower
Colchicum speciosum album 111 (4–9)
Color
fences 45
gates 56–7
perspective enhancement 17
planting schemes 32
walling materials 33
Compartments 28, 32, *32*
division *9, 11*
ground plans 10
style 19
Compost, siting 15
Concrete
block walls 36, 86
paving 63, 65, 68
posts, fences 45
walling materials 33
Conifers, pruning 52
Containers, steps 89
Convallaria majalis 78 (2–8)
Convolvulus elegantissimus **110** (6–8)
Copper beech *82*
Cornus see Dogwood
Corylus see Hazel
Cosmos 113
Costs
fences *42*
hard surfaces 62
paving materials 65
wall building 34–5
Cotinus coggygria 111, 113 (4–8)
Cotoneaster 55
C. horizontalis 39, 121 (5–7)
Cotton lavender (*Santolina chamaecyparissus*) 49, *79* (7–9)
Crambe cordifolia see Kale
Crataegus
C. laevigata 99, 119 (5–7)
C. lavallei 107 (4–8)
C. monogyna 48 (5–7)
Crazy paving 63
Creeping Jenny (*Lysimachia nummularia*) *91* (3–8)
Crocus
C. sativus 118 (5–8)
C. tommasinianus 83, 117, 118 (3–8)
Cup and saucer flower (*Cobaea scandens*) 39, *54,* 96, **120,**

121, 122 (9–11)
X *Cupressocyparis leylandii see* Leyland cypress
Curves
hard surfaces 60
measurement *20, 21*
Cut-in steps 88, *88*
Cyclamen coum 83 (5–8)
Cydonia oblonga 99 (4–8)
Cynara
C. cardunculus see Artichoke, Cardoon (6–8)
C. scolymus see Globe artichoke
Cynoglossum nervosum 91 (5–8)
Cytisus battandieri 74, 123 (8–9)

Daphne **116**
D. x burkwoodii 116, **116** (5–8)
D. odora 70, 74, **116** (7–9)
Deciduous screens 54
Decking 64
Delphinium (*Delphinium*) 110, 112, 113
Density, hedges/boundaries 30
Dianthus 16
D. caryophyllus 74 (7–9)
Dictamnus albus purpureus 101 (2–8)
Digitalis see Foxglove
Dipsacus fullonum see Teasel
Disguise
see also Screening
plot shape/size 16
Dog rose (*Rosa canina*) 50 (5–8)
Dogwood (*Cornus*) **116**
C. alba 39, 55, *55,* 81, **116** (2–7)
C. alternifolia 87 (4–7)
C. controversa 10, 87 (5–8)
C. mas **116** (4–8)
Drainage, paving preparation 66–7
Drawing, plans 22–3, *22*
Drives 80–1
materials 80
plants 80–1, *80*
pollution-tolerant plants 81
tarmac 65
Dryopteris filix-mas see Fern
Dry stone walls
construction 36, *37*
planting ideas *41*
Dusty miller vine *see* Grapevine
Dwarf box *see* Box

Earthworks *25*
Eccremocarpus

E. scaber aurantiacus 121 (8–9)
E. scabra 46 (8–9)
Elaeagnus x ebbingei 54, 81 (6–9)
Elder (*Sambucus*)
S. nigra 54, 55, 113, 115, *118,* **119** (4–9)
S. racemosa 116 (4–7)
Entrances 80–1
Eranthus 117
Erigeron karvinskianus 71, 77 (8–9)
Eryngium giganteum see Sea holly
Erysimum 'Bowles' Mauve' *78, 79* (6–9)
Escallonia 31
E. 'Donard Seedling' 50 (8–10)
Eucalyptus camphora 74 (8–10)
Euonymus
E. alatus see Spindle berry
E. fortunei 39, *70,* 81 (5–8)
E. fortunei radicans 45 (5–8)
Eupatorium maculatum **110–11** (3–8)
Euphorbia
E. amygdaloides robbiae 78 (5–9)
E. characias wulfenii see Spurge
E. x martinii 116 (7–9)
E. palustris 78 (7–9)
E. robbiae 87, 116 (7–9)
Evergreens
fences 45
hedges 50
screens 54
Everlasting pea (*Lathyrus*) **122** (6–9)
L. grandiflorus 41, 119, *122* (5–9)
L. latifolius **122** (5–9)
L. odoratus see Sweet pea
L. rotundifolius 46, 118, **122** (5–9)
L. vernus 115 (4–7)
Exotics, wall protection 38

Fagus sylvatica see Beech
Fallopia baldschuanica see Russian vine
Fatsia japonica 81 (7–9)
Features 94–101
plant-clad 100–1
plants 98–9, **114–15**
Fedges 44
Fences 29
chain link *47*

choice 42–4
climbing roses *28*
imaginative designs 31
iron estate 44
maintenance 44–5
panel fixing *43*
picket 43, *46*
planting ideas *46–7*
post and rail 44
post and wire 44
preservatives 45
vertical board *47*
wood slat and wire paling 44
woven 42–3, *46*
Fern (*Dryopteris filix-mas*) *91* (4–9)
Fern (*Polypodium vulgare*) *91,* 119 (5–8)
Fern (*Polystichum setiferum*) 40, 78 (4–9)
Fertilizer, hedges 51, 52
Feverfew 56
Ficus carica see Fig
Field maple (*Acer campestre*) 50 (5–8)
Fig (*Ficus carica*) *21,* 39, 98 (8–10)
Filipendula rubra 115 (3–8)
Flag iris (*Iris pallida*) *7, 18, 37* (6–9)
Flame creeper (*Tropaeolum speciosum*) 50, 121 (7–9)
Floating features, measurement *20, 21*
Focal points 11, 29
Foeniculum vulgare 101, 113 (4–9)
Formal gardens 60
Foundations
paved areas *66*
wall building 34, *34,* 35
Fountains 94, *95*
Foxglove (*Digitalis*)
D. purpurea 41, 112, 113, 118 (4–8)
D. purpurea alba 114 (4–8)
Fritillaria imperialis 105 (5–8)
Fruit, wall protection 38–9
Fuchsia magellanica 78, 79 (7–9)

Galanthus 117
G. nivalis 83 (3–8)
Garden features 94–101
Garden "rooms" *see* Themes
Garden sheds, siting 15
Garrya elliptica 39, *41, 70* (7–9)
Gate posts 57
Gates 56–7, *56, 57*
Gaultheria 18
Gaura lindheimeri **111** (6–9)

Gazebos 29, 94
Gentiana asclepiadea see Willow gentian
Geranium 31
G. 'Claridge Druce' 31 (4–9)
G. grandiflorum 57 (5–8)
G. macrorrhizum 101 (3–8)
G. renardii 78 (6–8)
G. sylvaticum album 114 (4–8)
G. 'Wargrave Pink' 31 (4–9)
Gleditsia triacanthos 99 (4–9)
Globe artichoke (*Cynara scolymus*) 11 (6–8)
Golden hop (*Humulus lupulus* 'Aureus') *47, 94,* 96, *121* (5–9)
Granite blocks 63, 64
paths *77, 79*
paving 63, 64, 68, *69*
terraces *74*
Grapevine (*Vitis vinifera*) *33,* 39, *54,* 96, *100,* 118 (6–9)
Graph paper, drawing plans 23
Grass paths 76–7
Gravel 62
drives *80*
laying 69
paths *13,* 76, *76*
paving materials 64
paving preparation 67
plants 77
sunny area, midsummer *71*
Greenhouses, siting 15
Ground plan, development 10–11
Guelder rose (*Viburnum opulus*) 50 (3–8)

Hand pruners, hedge trimming 52
Hazel (*Corylus*)
C. avellana 50 (4–8)
C. maxima 113 (5–8)
Headers, bricks 36
Hebe 41, 71, 78, 79, 90, 116
H. buxifolia 70 (8–10)
H. 'Mrs. Winder' 78 (8–10)
H. 'Pewter Dome' 90, 115 (7–10)
H. pinguifolia 110 (7–10)
H. rakaiensis 115, 116 (7–10)
H. 'Red Edge' 41, 116 (8–10)
Hedera see Ivy
Hedges
boundary/dividing 29, 48–52
choice 48–51
clipping 48, 52
establishment 24
flowering/fruiting 49
imaginative designs 31
maintenance 52
mixed genus 50–1

planting 51
problems 52
single genus 48–9
trimmers 52
Height
boundaries 30
creation 96–7
internal divisions 32
Helianthemum 14
Helichrysum petiolare 115
(9–10)
Helictotrichon sempervirens 115
(4–9)
Hellebore (*Helleborus*) 114–15
H. argutifolius 114, 115 (6–8)
H. foetidus 41, 70, 114, 116,
117 (4–8)
H. orientalis 18, 117 (5–8)
Hemerocallis 31
Herb gardens *95*
Herringbone pattern, paving
64
Hesperis matronalis 74 (3–8)
Holly (*Ilex*) 50, 99, *103*
I. × altaclerensis 121 (7–9)
I. aquifolium 48, 50, 81 (7–9)
Honeysuckle (*Lonicera*) **122**
L. japonica 45, *46*, 96, 121,
122 (5–9)
L. nitida 9, *31*, 49, 116, 121
(7–9)
L. periclymenum see
Woodbine
L. pileata 81 (6–8)
Hop *see* Golden hop
Horizontal dimension 59–91
Hornbeam (*Carpinus*) 98, *98*
C. betulus 48, 50 (5–8)
Hosta 40, *78*
H. fortunei 121 (3–9)
H. 'Francee' 40 (3–9)
H. plantaginea 116 (3–9)
H. plantaginea grandiflora 111
(3–9)
H. 'Thomas Hogg' 116 (3–9)
Houses, garden integration *13*,
17, *17*, 60
Hover mowers 85
Humea elegans 74 (annual)
Humulus lupulus 'Aureus' see
Golden hop
Hydrangea
H. anomala petiolaris see
Climbing hydrangea
H. arborescens 9, 111, 116
(4–9)
H. macrophylla 81, *93* (6–9)
H. paniculata 121 (4–8)
H. seemannii 45 (9–10)
Hypericum calycinum 87 (6–8)

Ilex see Holly
Internal divisions *see*
Compartments
Ipomoea tricolor 120 (annual)
Iris
I. foetidissima 91, 115 (6–8)
I. pallida see Flag iris
Ironwork, arches *100*
Itea ilicifolia 38, 39 (7–9)
Ivy (*Hedera*) *34*, **120–1**
H. canariensis 47 (9–10)
H. colchica 45 (6–9)
H. helix 39, 41, 47, 54, 70, 91,
116, 119, **121** (5–9)
H. hibernica 40 (5–9)

Jackman's rue *see* Rue
Japanese crab apple (*Malus
floribunda*) 82, 98, 99, *117*,
117 (4–7)
Jasmine (*Jasminum*) **121**
J. nudiflorum see Winter
jasmine
J. officinale see Summer
jasmine
Jasminum see Jasmine
Jointing, paving 69
Judas tree (*Cercis siliquastrum*)
82 (6–9)
Juglans see Walnut

Kale (*Crambe cordifolia*) *110*,
110, 114, 115 (6–9)
Kalmia 18
Key stones, wall construction *37*
Kniphofia 32
Knotweed (*Persicaria*) **112**
P. affinis 112 (3–8)
P. amplexicaulis 112 (5–9)
P. bistorta 112 (3–8)
Kolwitzia amabilis 32 (5–9)

Laburnum × watereri 96 (6–7)
Lamium maculatum 91 (3–8)
Larch (*Larix decidua*) 55 (2–7)
Larix decidua see Larch
Lathyrus see Everlasting pea;
Sweet pea
Laurel *see* Cherry laurel
Laurus nobilis see Bay
Lavandula see Lavender
Lavatera 119
L. olbia see Mallow
Lavender (*Lavandula*) *13, 14, 32,
56*, 112
L. angustifolia 49, 74, *79, 90,
101* (7–9)
L. 'Hidcote' 4 (5–9)
L. stoechas see Spanish
lavender

Lawn mowers 85
Lawns 82–5
feasibility 62
ground plans 10, 14
laying 83
maintenance 83, 84–5
shaping 84
size 82
Layout
planning 13–25
testing 24
Leucanthemum Vulgare 84 (3–9)
Level changes *23*, 86–7
Lewisia tweedyi 74 (6–7)
Leyland cypress
(X *Cupressocyparis leylandii*)
49, 75 (6–9)
Light, internal divisions 32
Ligularia dentata 115 (4–8)
Ligustrum ovalifolium see Privet
Lilium 'Côte d'Azur' 74 (3–8)
Linaria purpurea 71 (4–9)
Linden (*Tilia*) *21*, 98
T. × euchlora 81 (4–7)
Linum perenne 57 (5–9)
Local materials, boundaries 31
Lonicera see Honeysuckle
Lysimachia
L. nummularia see Creeping
jenny
L. punctata 80 (4–9)

Magnolia
M. grandiflora 39, 121, **122**
(7–9)
M. wilsonii 82 (6–8)
Mahonia 54
M. lomariifolia 45 (8–9)
M. × media 81 (7–8)
Maintenance
fences 44–5
garden planning 14
hedges 52
lawns 83, 84–5
seasonal 103–7
style effects 19
Mallow (*Lavatera olbia*) 54
(7–10)
Malus 98
M. floribunda see Japanese
crab apple; Ornamental
crab apple
M. hupehensis 81 (4–8)
Malva sylvestris 9 (5–8)
Materials
boundaries 31
fences 42–4
house influence 17, *17*
paving *61*, 63–5
steps 88–9

walls 33
Matteuccia struthiopteris 78
(2–8)
Matthiola incana 101 (annual)
Meadow rue (*Thalictrum*) 113
T. aquilegiifolium 110, **113**
(5–8)
T. dipterocarpum 38 (5–8)
T. flavum glaucum 113 (5–9)
Measurement, site 20–1
Meconopsis cambrica see
Welsh poppy
Melianthus major 39, 79, 115
(7–10)
Mespilus germanica 99 (5–8)
Mexican orange blossom
(*Choisya ternata*) *39, 45, 47,
74*, 116 (7–9)
Microclimates
description 18
site orientation 19
Mock orange (*Philadelphus*) 120
P. coronarius 39, 74, 101, **118**
(4–7)
P. microphyllus 27 (6–8)
Monarda 'Croftway Pink' 114
(4–9)
Mortar, wall joints 36
Morus nigra see Black mulberry
Moss, lawns 85
Mowers 85
Mowing edges 61, 76, 84
Mulberry *see* Black mulberry
Mullein (*Verbascum*) 113
V. olympicum 71, 77, 113, **113**
(6–8)
V. phoeniceum 113 (6–8)
Myrrhis odorata 74 (4–9)
Myrtle (*Myrtus communis*) 74
(8–9)

Narcissus 70, 115, 116
N. 'February Gold' 115 (3–8)
N. 'Peeping Tom' 116 (38)
N. poeticus recurvus 117
(4–8)
N. 'Tête-à-Tête' 70 (3–8)
Natural stone 63
Nectaroscordum 117 (7–10)
Nepeta see Catmint
Nerine bowdenii 111 (7–9)
Nicotiana
N. affinis 74 (annual)
N. sylvestris 101 (annual)

Oemleria cerasiformis see Oso
berry
Oenothera biennis 77, 113
(annual, biennial)
Onopordum acanthium see

Scotch thistle
Organic matter
hedges 51, 52
soils 18
Orientation, house/garden
18–19
Ornamental cabbage (*Brassica
oleracea*) 70 (annual)
Ornamental crab apple (*Malus
floribunda*) 82, 98, 99, *117*,
117 (4–7)
Ornamental pear (*Pyrus*) 118
P. calleryana 99, 118 (5–8)
P. nivalis 99, 118 (6–8)
Ornamental rhubarb (*Rheum
palmatum*) 10, 115 (5–9)
Osmanthus delavayii 49 (7–9)
Oso berry (*Oemleria
cerasiformis*) 41, 115, **117**
(6–9)

Paeonia see Peony
Painting
fences 45
gates 56–7
Papaver see Poppy
Parrotia persica 118 (5–8)
Parthenocissus tricuspidata see
Virginia creeper
Passiflora caerulea see Passion
flower
Passion flower (*Passiflora
caerulea*) 41, 45 (8–10)
Paths *65, 66*, 75–9
grass 76–7
materials 76–7
planting ideas 77, *78–9*
size 75
Paulownia tomentosa 54 (5–9)
Paved areas *59*, 70–4
Paving 60–74
base laying *67*
bedding the slabs *67*
laying 68–9
lichens/algae/moss *62*, 104
low-growing plants 77
man-made 65
materials *61*, 63–5
preparation 66–7
Pea gravel/shingle, paths 76
Pebbles, paving materials 63,
64, *64*
Penstemon 78, 79
Peony (*Paeonia*) 111
P. delavayi ludlowii 111 (6–8)
P. suffruticosa 111, **111** (4–7)
Pergolas *29, 38*, 96–7, *97*
building *96*
plants 96, *100*
Perovskia 79, 90

P. atriplicifolia see Russian sage

Persicaria see Knotweed

Perspective enhancement, color 17

pH, soil types 18

Philadelphus see Mock orange

Phlox 38

Pieris 18

Pittosporum tenuifolium 45 (8–10)

Plans
development 10–11, 20–1
drawing 22–3, *22*
priorities *24–5*
testing 24

Pleaching 98, *98–9*

Plots
assessment 16–19
measurements 20–1

Pointing walls 36

Pollarding 98–9

Pollution-tolerant plants 81

Polygonatum × hybridum see Solomon's seal

Polypodium vulgare see Fern

Polystichum setiferum see Fern

Ponds 15, 94–5

Pools, paved gardens *59*

Poplar (*Populus*)
P. alba 54, 116 (4–8)
P. balsamifera 74 (2–7)

Poppy (*Papaver*) *112*
P. orientale 78, *79*, *112* (3–7)

Populus see Poplar

Posts
erection *42*
fence maintenance 44–5
gates 57

Primula
P. auricula 74 (4–7)
P. japonica 110 (4–7)

Privacy, boundaries 30

Privet (*Ligustrum ovalifolium*), hedges 48, 49 (6–9)

Pruning
hedges 48, 52
winter maintenance 104

Prunus
P. armeniaca see Apricot
P. 'Kanzan' 105 (5–8)
P. laurocerasus see Cherry laurel
P. lusitanica 104 (7–9)
P. spinosa see Blackthorn
P. × subhirtella 99 (6–8)

Pulmonaria angustifolia 78 (3–8)

Pulsatilla 18

Pyracantha rogersiana flava 39 (7–9)

Pyrus see Ornamental pear

Quince (*Chaenomeles speciosa*) 39, 81 (5–8)

Railings
iron 29, *30*, 43–4

Raised beds 87

Rambling roses 45

Raoulia australis 77 (7–9)

Retaining walls 36, 86, *86*, 87, *87*

Rheum palmatum see Ornamental rhubarb

Rhododendron 18

Rhus
R. glabra 81 (3–9)
R. typhina 115 (4–8)

Ribes sanguineum 55 (5–7)

Rolling, lawns 85

Romneya coulteri 71 (7–10)

Rope-twist clay tiles *76*

Rosa see Rose

Rose (*Rosa*) 113, 118, 119
R. 'Alchymist' 66 (5–9)
'Ballerina' *79* (5–9)
R. banksiae 7, 38, *100*, 121, 122 (7–9)
'Blush rambler' 96 (4–9)
R. canina see Dog rose
'Constance Spry' *28*, 122 (5–9)
R. 'Dorothy Perkins' 41 (5–9)
dry stone walls *41*
R. eglanteria see Sweet brier
'Ena Harkness' 74 (5–9)
R. 'Fantin Latour' 113 (5–9)
R. glauca 110, 111, 115, 119 (2–8)
R. longicuspis 96, *100* (8–10)
R. 'Madame Gregoire Staechelin' 33 (5–9)
R. multiflora 43 (5–9)
R. 'Nevada' 32, 119 (5–9)
'Rambling Rector' 97 (4–9)
R. rugosa 49 (3–8)
R. 'Sanders White' 100 (5–9)
R. soulieana 115 (7–9)
R. 'The Fairy' 21 (5–9)
R. 'Zephirine Drouhin' 63, 122 (5–9)

Rosemary (*Rosmarinus officinalis*) 49, 74, *101* (6–10)

Rubus
R. cockburnianus 81 (5–8)
R. ulmifolius 38 (7–9)
R. 'Veilchenblau' 118 (5–9)

Rue (*Ruta*) 116
R. graveolens 41, 74, *79*, *101* (4–9)

Running bond, paving *64*, 68

Russian sage (*Perovskia atriplicifolia*) 112, **112** (5–9)
P. 'Blue Spire' *90* (5–9)

Russian vine (*Fallopia baldschuanica*) 54, 55 (5–8)

Ruta graveolens see Rue

Safety, ponds 15

Sage (*Salvia officinalis*) 74, *78*, *79*, *101*, 112, 119 (4–9)

Sagina subulata 77 (6–9)

Salix see Willow

Salt spray resistance, hedges 50

Salvia
S. officinalis see Sage
S. sclarea 113 (annual)
S. sclarea turkestanica 11, *71*, 77, **112–13** (biennial)

Sambucus see Elder

Sand pit *14*

Santolina 112
S. chamaecyparissus see Cotton lavender

Sarcococca see Sweet box

Sasa veitchii 87 (6–10)

Scarifying lawns 85, *85*

Scent
terraces 74
themes 32

Schizandra rubrifolia 96 (7–9)

Scotch thistle (*Onopordum acanthium*) *71*, 77, 110, **115** (biennial)

Screens 53–5, *53*
fast-growing plants *54*
offending structures 17

Sculpture 96

Sea holly (*Eryngium giganteum*) *71*, 77, **110** (5–8)

Seasonal planting 103–7

Seats 94, 96, *101*

Sedum 78
S. acre 77 (3–9)
S. maximum *79* (3–9)
S. 'Ruby Glow' 78 (5–8)
S. spectabile *79* (4–9)

Seed, lawn laying 83

Shears, hedge trimming 52

Shrubs **116–19**
see also Wall shrubs
screening 55
vertical dimension 29

Silene fimbriata see White-fringed campion

Sinarundinaria nitida see Bamboo

Sisyrinchium striatum 77, 110 (6–8)

Sites
see also Plots

garden features 94
terraces 72–3

Skimmia japonica 81, *91* (7–9)

Slopes 86

Smilacina racemosa 78 (3–7)

Smyrnium perfoliatum *91* (5–8)

Snowball tree (*Viburnum opulus*) 119, **119** (3–8)

Sod, lawn laying 83, *83*

Soils
improvement 18, *24*
structure 18
texture 18
type, assessment 18

Solanum **122–3**
S. crispum 45, 54, *100*, **123** (8–10)
S. jasminoides *100*, **123** (7–10)
wall protection 38

Soleirolia soleirolii 77, *91* (8–10)

Solomon's seal (*Polygonatum × hybridum*) 40, *78*, 114 (3–9)

Sorbus 98
S. 'Joseph Rock' 107 (6–8)

Spanish lavender (*Lavandula*)
L. stoechas *79* (8–9)
L. stoechas pedunculata *71* (8–9)

Spindle berry (*Euonymus alatus*) 50 (5–9)

Spiraea arguta 14 (4–8)

Spirit levels *66*

Spring, garden maintenance 104

Spurge (*Euphorbia characias wulfenii*) *71*, 113, **114** (7–10)

Stachys byzantina *79* (4–8)

Statues *93*, 96

Stepping stones, laying 68–9

Steps 88–91
containers 89
cut-in 88, *88*
freestanding *89*
materials 88–9
plants 89
planting plans *90–1*

Stipa gigantea 115 (7–8)

Stone paving
laying 68
materials 63–4
slabs *69*

Stone walls 33, *34*, 35–6, *36*, *37*

Stretcher bond *34*

Stretchers, bricks 36

Style, planting 19

Summer, garden maintenance 106

Summer houses 29, 94

Summer jasmine (*Jasminum*

officinale) 54, 96, *100*, **121** (8–10)

Surfaces 59–62

Sweet box (*Sarcococca*)
S. confusa 74 (7–8)
S. humilis 41, 116 (6–8)

Sweet brier (*Rosa eglanteria*) 49, 74, *101*, **118–19** (4–9)

Sweet pea (*Lathyrus odoratus*) 55, 97, *101* (annual)

Syringa 120
S. vulgaris 119 (4–7)

Tanacetum vulgare see Tansy

Tansy (*Tanacetum vulgare*) 74, 119 (3–9)

Taxus baccata 123 (6–7)

Teasel (*Dipsacus fullonum*) 9 (biennial)

Terraces 70–4
integration *72*, *73*
paving 62
planting ideas 74
planting plans *70–1*
siting 73

Teucrium × lucidrys see Wall germander

Thalictrum see Meadow rue

Themes, garden rooms 32

Thuja plicata 54 (5–7)

Thymus
T. serpyllum *71*, 77 (4–9)
T. vulgaris *101* (7–9)

Tiarella cordifolia 78 (3–8)

Tilia see Linden

Topiary 99

Trachelospermum jasminoides 39, 44 (7–9)

Tree of heaven (*Ailanthus altissima*) 54 (5–8)

Tree peony *see* Peony

Trees **116–19**
lawns 84
screening 55
small gardens 99
vertical dimension 29

Trellis
climbers *38*
screening 53, 54, *55*

Trenches, digging 51, *51*

Trimmers 85

Trimming, hedges 48, 52

Trompe l'oeil techniques 54–5

Tropaeolum
T. peregrinum 54 (9–10)
T. speciosum see Flame creeper

Tulipa
T. 'China Pink' 111 (4–8)
T. 'West Point' 111 (4–8)

Ulmus × hollandica **119** (5–6)
Urns 94, 96
Uvularia grandiflora 91 (5–8)

Valeriana phu· 70 (5–9)
Vegetable plots 15
Verbascum see Mullein
Verbena **113**
  V. bonariensis 110, 111, **113**
    (7–10)
Vertical dimension 27–57
Viburnum 45, 54
  V. carlesii 74 (5–7)
  V. henryi 45 (7–8)
  V. opulus see Guelder rose;
    Snowball tree
  V. 'Park Farm Hybrid' 45 (5–8)
  V. plicatum 87 (5–8)
  V. 'Pragense' 45 (6–8)
  V. tinus 49 (8–10)
Vinca
  V. major 87 (5–8)

V. minor 70 (5–8)
Vine-eyes, wall supports 38
Viola
  V. cornuta 79, 90 (6–8)
  V. labradorica 79, 93 (3–8)
Virginia creeper (Parthenocissus
  tricuspidata) 54 (4–9)
Vitis 123
  V. coignetiae 32, 54, 93, 123,
    123 (5–9)
  V. vinifera see Grapevine

Wall fountains 94, 95
Wall germander
  (Teucrium × lucidrys) 49 (4–9)
Wall shrubs 38–9, **120–3**
Walls 27, 33–41
  aspect 38–9
  bonds 34
  cobb 33, 34
  cold, plants 39, 39
  construction 34–7, 34

coping 36–7, 36, 37
  paint-decorated 54
  planting plans 40–1
  shady, plants 38–9, 40, 41
  wall supports 38
  warm, plants 38–9, 39, 41
Walnut (Juglans) 11, **116–17**
  J. nigra 117 (5–9)
  J. regia 117 (5–9)
Water, garden features 15,
  94–5, 94
Wattle fences 43, 43, 45
Weeds, eradication 24
Weigela florida 55, 78, 79 (5–8)
Welsh poppy (Meconopsis
  cambrica) 40 (annual)
White-fringed campion (Silene
  fimbriata) 91 (5–8)
Willow fedges 44
Willow gentian (Gentiana
  asclepiadea) 91 (5–8)
Willow (Salix) 55, 98

S. alba 54 (3–8)
S. purpurea 99, 111 (4–7)
Wind protection
  boundaries 31
  fences 43
  gates 56
  hedges 48, 50
Winter, garden maintenance
  104
Winter jasmine (Jasminum
  nudiflorum) 39, 47, 54, **121**
  (5–10)
Winter sweet (Chimonanthus
  praecox) 39, 74 (6–7)
Wire mesh, wall supports 38
Wisteria 13, 114, **123**
  W. floribunda 39, 96, 100,
    109, 120, 123, **123** (5–9)
  W. sinensis 45, 54, 74, 122,
    123 (5–8)
Wood
  paving materials 64, 64

steps 89, 89
Wood chippings
  laying 69
  paving materials 64
Woodbine (Lonicera
  periclymenum) 39, 55, 74,
  100, **122** (4–8)
Wooden posts
  erection 42
  maintenance 44–5
Wrought-iron gates 56, 56

Yew (Taxus baccata)
  hedges 8, 10, 15, 23, 32, 50,
    103 (6–7)
  topiary 99
  watering 48
Yucca 98, **115**
  Y. gloriosa 90, **115** (6–9)

Acknowledgments

Author's acknowledgments

The subject of garden design is so broad that it presented a daunting prospect when I first sat down to write this book. I was therefore very grateful for the expertise offered by the team at Conran Octopus, guiding me in the right direction and helping me to keep a sense of proportion. The illustrator, Shirley Felts, has my sincere thanks and admiration for bringing to life borders and plant combinations that existed only in my imagination.

I owe a debt of gratitude to the staff of The Royal Horticultural Society garden at Wisley and of the Royal Botanic Gardens, Kew, England, for the great fund of knowledge they imparted to their students. I would also like to thank Rosemary Verey for her help and encouragement, my clients for their patience and, finally, my parents for their support.

Publisher's acknowledgments

The publisher thanks the following photographers and organizations for their kind permission to reproduce the photographs in this book.

1 S&O Mathews; 2–3 Ron Sutherland/The Garden Picture Library (Michael Balston Design); 4–5 Christine Ternynck (Huys de Dom); 6–7 Hugh Palmer: IPC Magazines Ltd/ Robert Harding Syndication; 8 Michael Boys/Boys Syndication; 9 left Andrew Lawson; 9 right Brigitte Perdereau; 10 Clive Nichols (Little Bowden, Berkshire); 11 above Georges Lévêque (Mr. and Mrs. Verstraten, Zaamslag); 11 below John Glover; 12–13 Brigitte Perdereau; 14 Christine Ternynck; 15 above Brigitte Perdereau; 15 below Eric Crichton Photos; 16 above Jerry Harpur/Elizabeth Whiting & Associates; 16 below Marianne Majerus; 17 Ron Sutherland/The Garden Picture Library; 19 Christine Ternynck; 21 Georges Lévêque (Mr. and Mrs. Joyaux, Jardin privé à Crissay-sur Manse); 22 Christine Ternynck; 26–7 Marianne Majerus/The Garden Picture Library; 30 Clive Nichols (Malvern Terrace, London); 32 Brigitte Perdereau/ The Garden Picture Library; 33 Rob Judges: IPC Magazines Ltd/Robert Harding Syndication; 34 Clive Nichols (Heale House, Wiltshire); 35 Hugh Palmer; 37 Eric Crichton Photos; 39 Marianne Majerus; 43 Neil Holmes; 44 left Andrew Lawson; 44 right Eric Crichton Photos; 45 Marianne Majerus; 49 above Christine Ternynck; 49 below Christine Ternynck; 50 Jerry Harpur (House of Pitmuies, Guthrie-by-Forfar); 51 above Christine Ternynck; 51 below Christine Ternynck; 53 Andrew Lawson; 54 Marianne Majerus; 55 left Annette Shreiner; 55 right Michèle Lamontagne; 56 Hugh Palmer; 57 Michael Boys: IPC Magazines Ltd/Robert Harding Syndication; 58–9 Gary Rogers/The Garden Picture Library; 61 above Marianne Majerus; 61 below Brigitte Perdereau; 62 Hugh Palmer: IPC Magazines Ltd/Robert Harding Syndication; 63 Michael Boys/Boys Syndication; 65 left Jerry Tubby/ Elizabeth Whiting & Associates; 65 right Christine Ternynck; 66 Marianne Majerus; 68 Photos Horticultural; 69 above John Glover/The Garden Picture Library; 69 below Eric Crichton Photos; 72 Eric Crichton Photos; 73 Ron Sutherland/The Garden Picture Library; 74 Eric Crichton Photos; 75 Hugh Palmer: IPC Magazines Ltd/Robert Harding Syndication; 76 above John Glover; 77 John Glover/The Garden Picture Library; 80 Jerry Harpur; 81 Gary Rogers/The Garden Picture Library; 82 Jerry Harpur/ Elizabeth Whiting & Associates; 83 Andrew Lawson; 84 James Merrell: IPC Magazines Ltd/Robert Harding Syndication; 87 Jerry Harpur; 89 left Eric Crichton Photos; 89 right Noel Kavanagh; 92–3 Clive Nichols (Osler Road, Oxford); 94 Andrew Lawson; 95 Brigitte Perdereau; 97 above Jerry Harpur (Hazleby House); 97 below Brigitte Perdereau; 98 Marianne Majerus; 102–3 Clive Nichols (Wollerton Old Hall, Shropshire); 104 Clive Nichols (The Winter Garden, University Botanic Garden, Cambridge); 105 Neil Holmes; 106 Jerry Tubby/Elizabeth Whiting & Associates; 107 Rob Judges: IPC Magazines Ltd/Robert Harding Syndication; 108–9 Vaughan Fleming/The Garden Picture Library; 110 Brigitte Perdereau/The Garden Picture Library; 112 Andrew Lawson; 113 Jerry Harpur (Denmans); 116 Andrew Lawson; 118 Didier Willery/The Garden Picture Library; 119 Andrew Lawson; 120 John Glover/The Garden Picture Library; 122 Michael Boys/ Boys Syndication; 123 Andrew Lawson.

The publisher also thanks: Lesley Craig, Helen Ridge, Barbara Nash and Janet Smy.

Index compiled by Indexing Specialists, Hove, East Sussex BN3 2DJ, England.